D1065163

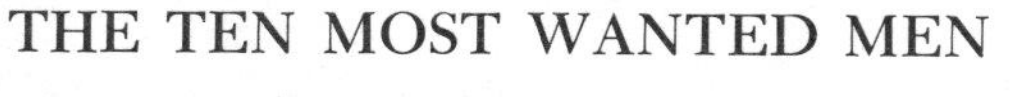

THE TEN MOST WANTED MEN

THE TEN MOST WANTED MEN

by
PAUL H. DUNN

BOOKCRAFT
Salt Lake City, Utah

LIBRARY OF CONGRESS CATALOG CARD NUMBER 67-17928

13th Printing, 1977

LITHOGRAPHED BY
PUBLISHERS PRESS

SALT LAKE CITY, UTAH
UNITED STATES OF AMERICA

DEDICATION

To my wife Jeanne and daughters Janet, Marsha and Kellie for the eternal joy and happiness they bring.

PREFACE

P. T. Barnum was, among other things, a great showman. "The greatest lesson I ever learned," he said, "was that everything depended on getting people to think, talk and become curious and excited about you." In short, he had stumbled upon the important secret of any success story—YOU!

Researchers make an endless game of trying to narrow down and single out the elements uniquely present in the lives of those who have achieved success. Their findings, while interesting and useful, are anything but unanimous. However on this point they all agreed—*you are unique. You* are an individual unlike any other. *You* are your own program for success. *You* are the key to successful leadership.

The success of any program is in direct proportion to the person or persons given the responsibility to lead. A Sunday School class is no better than the learning and inspiration which are experienced there. A leadership meeting is not much better than the planning and execution of the program involved therewith. If the Church is to accomplish all that the Lord intends it should, it will be because *you,* the leader, *you,* the teacher, and *you,* the member, are the machines which make it run.

That is what this book is all about—how to become more effective in leadership positions. It is really three books in one: 1. The right-hand page carries the text —principle material; 2. The left-hand page carries stories, quotes and inspirational thoughts which illustrate the principle on the right-hand page; 3. The entire book carries "program learning" exercises. Throughout the various chapters you will note the many opportunities to test yourself on the principles discussed.

The creation of any work involves many people. Appreciation is given to the countless hundreds of leaders and teachers throughout the Church who through their vision, skill and dedication have led the way; a special "thanks" to William O. Nelson for his many suggestions and ideas which have been incorporated; to Richard L. Gunn for his outstanding illustrations; to Dale T. Tingey for constant encouragement and inspiration; to Velma Harvey, my able secretary, for usual "extra mile" efforts in typing manuscripts, proofreading and following through on the many details necessary in preparing this book for publication; to my wife, Jeanne, I am eternally grateful for making "all things possible" through true devotion and constant sacrifice.

—Paul H. Dunn

Salt Lake City, Utah
December 18, 1966

CONTENTS

Chapter 1

WANTED THE MAN WHO WORKS WITH GOD

At the completion of this chapter, you should be able to:

1. Explain how you can improve your relationship with God.

2. Explain how you can improve your relationship with God by caring for your fellow men.

3. Explain how you can improve your relationship with God by your dedication to the building of his kingdom.

Chapter 1

THE MAN WHO WORKS WITH GOD

Establishing a Right Relationship with God

Over 2,000 years ago, when questioned by one of the scribes, Jesus gave an important directive that defined man's relationship to God in these words:

> Thou shalt *love the Lord thy God* with all thy heart, and with all thy soul, and with all thy mind, and with all thy strength: this is the first commandment. And the second is like, namely this, Thou shalt *love thy neighbour as thyself.* (Mark 12:30-31.)

From this divine injunction, we may conclude that any man who professes to work with God must have an established relationship with God in terms of (1) himself, (2) others, (3) the Father's kingdom.

The workability of this principle is demonstrated in the autobiography of Enos. He found that a man moves outside of the circle of concern for his own soul only when he has satisfied his own relationship with God. It then became his desire to minister the gospel to his friends, and finally to his enemies. Three selective verses illustrate this transition:

> And my soul hungered; and I kneeled down before my Maker, and I cried unto him in mighty prayer

Seek ye the Lord while he may be found, call ye upon him while he is near: Let the wicked forsake his way, and the unrighteous man his thoughts: and let him return unto the Lord, and he will have mercy upon him; and to our God, for he will abundantly pardon. For my thoughts are not your thoughts, neither are your ways my ways, saith the Lord. For as the heavens are higher than the earth, so are my ways higher than your ways, and my thoughts than your thoughts.

—Isa. 55:6-9

and supplication for *mine own soul;* and all the day long did I cry unto him; yea, and when the night came I did still raise my voice high that it reached the heavens. . . . Now, it came to pass that when I had heard these words I began to feel a desire for the welfare *of my brethren,* the Nephites; wherefore, I did pour out my whole soul unto God for them. . . . And after I, Enos, had heard these words, my faith began to be unshaken in the Lord; and I prayed unto him with *many long strugglings for my brethren, the Lamanites.* (Enos 4-11.)

A right relationship with God can thus be summarized in this way: It is a relationship in which a man works with God over his own soul, then feels a concern for the souls of his loved ones, and finally ministers to mankind. How this can be accomplished is the theme of this chapter.

How to Improve Your Relationship with God

Getting Answers to Prayers

Generally, there are three kinds of workers in the Church, using preparation and nonpreparation as the basis of classification. One group feels that the mental endowment and capacity they have been blessed with is all that is needed to fulfil their responsibility. They prepare without any thought of divine guidance.

Another group leaves everything to the Lord which usually means reliance on the impulse of the moment and it is frequently mistaken for inspiration. Their resort is to place all their burdens on the Lord with the hope and expectation that he will solve their problems.

That is the very lesson I would like to teach, that *prayer is the time you make your decisions.* You decide between the central issue which so masters life—the approval of God on the one hand, or the approval of man upon the other. That is where you fight; that is your private battlefield, until you have made up your own mind. Or else you will discover, if you do not fight it on that battlefield, and win victoriously in a private way all by yourself and with your God, that as you move out into the public battlefields of life you will buckle under the pressures upon you. Things will pull you apart—strong, unstable personalities, temptations, other buffeting experiences—and you will be uprooted and torn, and you may tend to compromise, to lower your standards. Then you gradually lose your integrity and the sense of who you are, the covenant children of the Lord.

—Steven Covey, in talk to students at BYU, February 22, 1966, *Build on the True Foundation—Christ in you.*

Neither of these approaches is adequate. The first is one of self-sufficiency. It exalts the resources of man, which is commendable, but allows no opportunity for the Spirit of the Lord to work with man since he feels independent of the need for help. The second approach is one of complete dependency. It exalts the resources of God, which is most praiseworthy, but allows no opportunity for the growth and development of the individual since he feels so unworthy and incapable.

The third group (the one which should be our example) shows how a personal relationship with God can be acquired. The individuals in this group have a great respect for their own resources and capabilities, but realize that the Spirit of the Lord is needed to magnify their own abilities. We have often heard the idea expressed that two people can do anything as long as one of them is the Lord.

The leader who works with the Lord will realize that when he accepts a call to serve, he is being called, not to do his own work, but to assist God with his work.

The story is told that during a heated battle, one of Lincoln's generals, knowing that Lincoln was a religious man, suggested that he hoped the Lord was on their side. The general must have learned a great lesson that day as Lincoln replied: "I don't care whether he is or isn't! I just hope we are on the Lord's side." God did a great work through Joseph Smith, and there isn't any person called to serve who has any greater challenge than did the Prophet. This should give comfort to those of us who might feel that we are not capable of meeting the challenge of our assignment. If we work with the Lord, he will help prepare us and we will succeed. God wants to do a "marvelous work" through each of us. To receive a call in the Church is to receive a vote of confidence from the Lord which is worthy of our deepest devotion to service.

"The things of God are of deep import; and time and experience and careful and ponderous and solemn thoughts can only find them out. Thy mind, O Man, if thou wilt lead a soul unto salvation, must stretch as high as the utmost heavens and search into and contemplate the darkest abyss and the broad expanse of eternity—*thou must commune with God!*"

—Joseph Smith

Doing the work of God does not reduce one to a mere "errand boy" wherein he does nothing until specifically instructed. Therefore, the effectiveness of the person who works with God will depend upon the extent of his own creativity in constantly improving his approach, methods and techniques in working with people.

The work of an MIA leader is impressive. First of all, the stake leader attends the MIA June Conference in Salt Lake City where she catches the general vision and spirit of the program that is outlined and presented by the General Board. She then proceeds to become acquainted with the details of the total program for the entire year. Each lesson, activity, goal, and objective is reviewed so that proper perspective is established. In other words, up to this point the leader has been placing herself on the side of the Lord.

Her program has now become her own, and at that point an amazing thing begins to happen. The leader takes the materials received and breaks them down into meaningful parts. Mentally she tries everything. She searches through books, magazines, life experiences—everywhere to get ideas. The needs of the students and the needs and personality of every teacher working under her are carefully considered. As she does all this her heart is drawn out in prayer to God and then a "marvelous work" begins to take place. This leader, with the help of God, literally "creates" the presentation, the aids, the helps which she is to give to her teachers. Each presentation becomes a masterpiece of unity between the program from God and creative adaptation and interpretation into daily life by a teacher who lives with, understands, loves and desires to help her fellow men. They catch the spirit and "know-how" of what she has done and follow the same pattern in their individual responsibilities. She is a leader of men in the hands of God.

On a Western University campus, a junior student approached his minister to inquire about the eternal state of the Oriental students attending the university who were not "Christian." The reply he received, "Unless they accept Jesus as their Savior in their lifetime, I'm afraid they are lost," caused this inquiring student to look outside his own faith for answers to his questions.

The following summer, while playing semi-professional baseball, he came into contact for the first time with several Mormon boys. There was little attempt on their part to influence him into the Church because of their laxity in keeping certain standards of the Church. Through one of the young men, however, he came into contact with a family who was living the principles of the gospel in addition to their desire to share it with others. Over a period of three months of reading, studying and listening, he became very impressed with what they had to say. He had been counseled to read the Book of Mormon in the spirit of Moroni 10:4-5. Though his parents objected to his investigation, he continued to read and study. Frequently, he knelt down beside his bed and asked if the work and Book of Mormon was true. No answer came. After the period of interest and investigation on his part became evident to his parents, the ultimatum was given, "Either you choose the family or the Mormon Church. You can't choose the Mormon Church and remain in the family."

That night he went to his room and prayed again. This time, however, the prayer took on a different dimension. Where before he prayed for understanding and direction, now he HAD TO KNOW. Where before there was curiosity and wishing, now there was sincerity and real intent. At that point the answer came! As he has described in his testimony to others: "There was no outward manifestation that came to me. The only

Making the Right Choices

Leaders sometimes tend to neglect using the Spirit of the Lord, when actually it should *finalize* every decision. If we do all within our power to solve our problems and make the proper decisions, and then ask the Lord for confirmation and verification, we soon discover we never err in our plans and decisions. This great principle was clearly taught in an experience Oliver Cowdery had while he was assisting Joseph Smith with the translation of the Book of Mormon. Oliver desired to have the gift of translation, and was granted the privilege. In effect, his attempt to translate failed and the Lord withdrew the privilege from him. The reason for his failure was summed up as follows:

> Behold, you have not understood; you have supposed that I would give it unto you, when you took no thought save it was to ask me. But, behold, I say unto you, that you must study it out in your mind; then you must ask me if it be right, and if it is right I will cause that your bosom shall burn within you; therefore, you shall feel that it is right. But if it be not right you shall have no such feelings, but you shall have a stupor of thought that shall cause you to forget the thing which is wrong; therefore, you cannot write that which is sacred save it be given you from me. (D. & C. 9:7-9.)

The steps outlined by the Lord for translating ancient records are fully applicable in solving any other problem. Every man who would work with God ought to use the following steps:

1. Study the problem out in his own mind.

2. Come to a tentative conclusion (the best decision he can reach, based on his study).

3. Ask if his conclusion is right.

difference between this experience and all the others when I had inquired in prayer of the truthfulness of the Church was that this time I really had to know. I promised I would do anything—even forego my family ties if necessary. When I arose from my knees, where before there had been doubts, this time I knew, through a calm inner assurance, that the Mormon Church was the only true Church, and that Joseph Smith was a prophet of God."

Two weeks later he was baptized into the Church, which decision caused the family to temporarily ostracize him. Upon graduation he went on a mission for the Church and since that time has been called to serve in various positions of responsibility.

4. Receive answer through the Holy Ghost.

   a. If right—"your bosom shall burn within you" (feeling of confirmation and assurance; knowing; no doubts).

   b. If wrong—"you shall have a stupor of thought" (feeling of doubt and uncertainty).

All leaders and members of the Church need to learn this process of receiving and interpreting correctly the spirit as it comes from the Lord. It forms the very heart of the working relationship between man and God. But the individual needs to understand that he must make the first move. As James summed it up so well, "Submit yourselves therefore to God. . . . Draw nigh to God, and he will draw nigh to you." (Jas. 4:7-8.)

This principle of receiving help from the Lord is always the same, but the method or process involved will change with each experience. No two experiences will be exactly alike except in principle. We must always study it out to the best of our ability and the Lord will finalize. Whenever the principle is followed effectively, we can act with confidence and be assured of being in agreement with God.

Which of the following would best represent an honest and personal point of view concerning the establishing of a right relationship with God?

1. The Lord has blessed me with all the mental abilities necessary to be successful and expects that I be independent. (Turn to page 25.)

2. There is so little that I can do with my limited ability that I must rely solely on the Lord for his help. (Turn to page 25.)

3. I feel that the capacity is certainly within me to do well, but I know that I can do so much better with the Lord's help. (Turn to page 25.)

I am ready to confess that I am keyed up to a pretty high tension, and the only thing I am afraid of is that I will say just what I think, which would be unwise, no doubt.

I feel a good deal, or at least I imagine I do, like a man does when held up by a burglar and he is looking into the muzzle of a six-shooter. I would quietly and willingly hold my hands up, but during the time would think very profoundly of what I would do if given my liberty. We are in a similar position today, but all the men in the United States cannot prevent a man from thinking. There are not Apostles enough in the Church to prevent us from thinking and they are not disposed to do so; but some people fancy because we have the Presidency and Apostles of the Church they will do the thinking for us. There are men and women so mentally lazy that they hardly think for themselves. To think calls for effort, which makes some men tired and wearies their souls. Now, brethren and sisters, we are surrounded with such conditions that it requires not only thought, but the guidance of the Holy Spirit. Latter-day Saints, you must think for yourselves. No man or woman can remain in this Church on borrowed light.

—Elder J. Golden Kimball,
Conf. Rep., Apr. 1904, p. 28.

Did you say, "The Lord has blessed me with all the mental abilities necessary to be successful without going to him for help"?

There is no question but what the Lord has endowed each of his children with great mental ability. Your answer indicates that you place great value on your capability and the power "within you" to do an acceptable job. You might strengthen this quality even more by seeking his guidance to magnify the talents you already possess. In so doing, your power to do and to accomplish may be increased. (Turn to page 17.)

Did you say, "There is so little that I can do with my limited ability that I must rely solely on the Lord for his help"?

Humility is a wonderful attribute. You are to be commended. Doing the Lord's work, however, should not make one feel he is only an "errand boy" wherein he does nothing until specifically instructed, but one should also feel that he has something creatively to offer that the Lord can use. By improving in his techniques and methods, the effectiveness of the Lord's work is proportionately increased. (Turn to page 17.)

Did you say, "I feel that the capacity is certainly within me to do well, but I know that I can do so much better with the Lord's help"?

This would be my personal feeling also, since it recognizes the divinity and capacity within man, as well as the need he has for dependence on divine inspiration and guidance to assist him in his decision-making process. It is a process that allows people to think as well as be inspired. (Turn to page 27.)

A teacher was called to serve in a position involving teen-age students. The setting was anything but favorable since the previous teacher was literally forced from the same position because of inability to "handle" most of the boys and even some of the girls. The first meeting with the new teacher was a continuation of the same pattern as far as the students were concerned. Facing the class with a definite and well-prepared program produced nothing but mild chaos. Inwardly, the students knew what they had done. The pattern was not new to them and they anticipated the usual recourse of a teacher in this situation—condemnation of their actions.

When it didn't come, they were so shocked that it completely disarmed them, and they were left wondering what the next move of the teacher would be. The "next move" came that night when the teacher made a visit to the home of two of the "leaders." As they were called into a family setting, an attitude of "this is it" was clearly written on the faces of boys and parents alike. Similar visits had been made before; hence everyone was well-rehearsed and knew just what to expect. But this visit was different! For an hour and a half, there was a solid interchange of human interest events and background information about each person in the group. Likes, dislikes, special abilities and such were uncovered. *Nothing* had been said about the classroom situation. *A group of people had simply made friends one with another.* Since it had been discovered that one of the boys had special building ability, the teacher asked the boy to help him in a little project for the widowed mother of one of the other boys. Through his kindnness and sincere interest he soon developed a relationship with the class where they accorded to him the same respect and love.

How to Improve your Relationship with God by Caring for your Fellow Men

Sincere Concern

Sincerity and concern for others are basic ingredients in improving one's relationship with God. People seem to sense when there is a real concern for their souls, or when there is a feigned interest that stems from obligation to a duty. How can they tell? It's how you show your concern and interest. A leader need not compromise principles or standards in showing genuine concern. Whenever I think of these qualities I always think of a former bishop. His love and concern for youth was demonstrated in the "extra" things he did. The time and energy he expended in their behalf was always a living testimony to observers.

At this time, I was one of fifteen boys in a teachers quorum. I had a close friend in the quorum who was a challenge to any leader. Each Sunday sometime between opening exercises and the quorum meeting, my friend would find his way to the corner drugstore. After ordering the largest soft drink available, he would park himself between the magazine rack and the window and engage in his only literary diversion. Whenever he was not in quorum meetings the bishop would head for the drugstore. He stood over six feet in height, weighed well over 200 pounds, and had one of the most jovial personalities I've ever seen in one man. He would walk into that drugstore and immediately head toward the magazine rack where he would spot my friend. "Bill, you *rascal!*" he would shout good naturedly, "you know you're supposed to be in your quorum meeting! Put that magazine down and get back in

While serving as director of the Institute of Religion at the University of Southern California I had an opportunity to accept an assignment offered by that school to be a participant among many educators and religious leaders. There were some 2,000 people who were to be assembled at this education conference, discussing ways and means of curbing some of the problems facing our young people today. Most of us were new to each other. We were brought from all over the country.

The presidency of the university provided a very fine luncheon just prior to our conference presentations. I noticed, as I stepped into the dining area, that I had been placed right beside a man in full Navy uniform, a commander by rank. We had never met. As we took our places—they were so identified by the little place cards—he turned to me. (To my knowledge he had no way of knowing that I was a Mormon.) He said, "Mr Dunn, I would like to get acquainted with you." We shook hands and he said, "You're the Latter-day Saint, aren't you?"

I thought, "Good heavens! What have I done to tip my hand already?" I said, "Yes, how did you know?"

He said, "I noticed that you are not going to partake of that liquid." I had turned my cup over. There was the clue. I immediately, as we frequently do almost mechanically, started to defend my position. He said, as he interrupted me very quickly, "Look, I didn't inquire about your background to get a defense of your position." I then asked him why and he said, "I wanted to take this opportunity to salute you. May I?"

Now I was just a Pfc in World War II and that isn't a high rank. Any time a Navy commander wants to salute a private, I am not going to stop him. So I turned to him and said, "Yes, sir. Please go ahead."

there." "Aw, bishop," he would protest, but he always responded positively after the bishop put his arm around him and walked him back to the ward. On other occasions the bishop would meet Bill at the door when he was about to sneak out. "Bill, you're going to have to walk through me or over me. Which will it be?" "Not today bishop," Bill would say as he looked over his massive frame.

The reason this bishop was able to say what he did and have Bill respond in a positive way toward him was because of the genuine interest he had in the boy. He was a very successful and busy businessman, but he would be out on the ball diamond watching his priesthood "boys" or he would drop by the drugstore on days other than Sunday, and buy them a soft drink and just visit. As a result we would have listened to anything that man had to tell us because he was sincerely concerned and interested in each one of us.

An Effective Example

Another way the leader demonstrates his real intent and interest toward others is the way he represents the gospel by his own living. The effective example is by far the best missionary tool we have, and conversely the poor example is the most detrimental barrier to the progress of others.

The baseball world was shocked, several years ago by the untimely death of the all-star second baseman, Ken Hubbs, of the Chicago Cubs. Shortly after his tragic death, a Los Angeles television station filmed the life story of the 22-year-old Mormon boy who set an all-time record in baseball in accepting 418 chances without an error. In interviewing the former coaches and teammates of this young man, the one thing they remember the most was not his unusual playing ability,

Then he hurt my ego a little. He said, "Well, I don't mean you, personally. I mean the organization that you are representing today—the Latter-day Saint faith."

I was very inquisitive. I wanted to know why he had singled us out. As we sat down, I inquired. I said, "Why do you pay tribute to my Church?"

He said, "Very simple. In my assignment as a Navy commander I am in charge of the testing program for the United States Navy. But even prior to this I had an opportunity to travel all over the world. I have watched you people with keen interest." He was a sharp, capable leader, himself. He said, "Mr. Dunn, I don't know what it is about you people, but you have something that gets through to me. It's an air of confidence; it's an ideal; it's something that I can't quite put my finger on; but I'm convinced, that one day the country, in fact, this world, will look to you people for spiritual direction. I want to take this opportunity as a family man, as an educator, and as a member of the armed forces, to salute you, sir, and your Church for your wonderful standards and spiritual truths. It gives us all a sense of well-being just to know that such an organization exists."

but his remarkable character. His former little league coach said of him: "He meant a lot to the youth of Colton because I think he was an ideal that the other kids would like to reach. He set an ideal that other kids were always shooting for."

John Morrow, his former basketball coach, after eulogizing his accomplishments as an all-American football and basketball player in high school, said of his character:

> Ken was what you might call the ideal American youth. He was outstanding in sports, but he was outstanding in school work too. He was a leader. He was elected student body president here. He was a leader in Church. I can recall one time taking a trip to Tucson with Kenny and his parents to watch his older brother play football when the University of Arizona was playing BYU. On the way back, it was a Sunday morning, we had to stop in a little town in Arizona so that Ken could go to Church. He was this type of a boy. It's pretty hard to imagine a teen-age boy interrupting a trip just so he could go to church. And that's the kind of a boy he was.

An outstanding star and teammate, Ernie Banks speaks of him this way:

> He was very interested in young people. I noticed that often after the ball games he would never pass up a kid who would ask him for an autograph. Every kid who came out, Kenny stopped and signed the autograph for him, and even talked to the kid at length. His whole life was youngsters. He loved people. He spent a lot of time talking to everybody. We had lunch together in Philadelphia with a sports writer friend of his from Colton and he talked at length about different things of life. I think Kenny, all in all, for a young man, had all the aspects of

> life and living. He was happy and very free with everybody.
>
> Kenny never thought about race, creed, or color. He was the type of player that didn't care what a guy was . . . or what his religious belief as long as he believed it and was dedicated to that. He was always nice to all of us. All the negro players on the Cubs were most happy to be associated with Kenny because he was never bad or had any derogatory remarks to say about the Negro race.

The all-star third baseman of the Cubs, Ron Santo, remembers upon hearing of his death:

> Of course it was a big shock and myself, being religious, I had to go to a Priest and think this over. Such a wonderful boy as Ken Hubbs who didn't drink or smoke and just had a good time and enjoyed life, why did he have to be the one? It's hard to understand but I'm sure he's very happy. It was a big shock.
>
> When we went to Spring training, we had a meeting right off the bat. Bob Kennedy (manager) called us together and it was hard for him to go through the meeting; he was so hurt by talking about it. "I feel that all the ball players that knew Kenny know that if we mourned over him, he would feel hurt. He would feel that we should go out and put out a little more for him. That's the type of guy he was. And we know this. That's why we're going to go out and put out a little more for him instead of just mourning."

His manager, Bob Kennedy, paid him this tribute: "I have a boy Bob, age 12. I hope he can be just like Hubbs."

It has been said—I think quite profoundly—that

A seventeen-year-old boy was assigned as a ward teacher to the home of Joseph Smith. He later wrote this description of his visit:

I felt my weakness in visiting the Prophet and his family in the capacity of a teacher. I almost felt like shrinking from duty. Finally I went to his door and knocked, and in a minute the Prophet came to the door. I stood there trembling, and said to him:

"Brother Joseph, I have come to visit you in the capacity of a teacher, if it is convenient for you."

He said: "Brother William, come right in, I am glad to see you; sit down in that chair there and I will go and call my family in."

They soon came in and took seats. He then said, "Brother William, I submit myself and family into your hands," and then took his seat. "Now, Brother William," said he, "ask all the questions you feel like."

By this time all my fears and trembling had ceased, and I said, "Brother Joseph, are you trying to live your religion?"

He answered, "Yes."

I then said, "Do you pray in your family?"

He said, "Yes."

"Do you teach your family the principles of the gospel?"

He replied, "Yes, I am trying to do it."

"Do you ask a blessing on your food?"

He answered, "Yes."

"Are you trying to live in peace and harmony with all your family?"

"the only Bible some people read is the Bible of other's lives." Applied to church work, the most effective message the leader teaches is with the way he lives the gospel. Alma stressed the importance of this over 2,000 years ago when he counseled:

> . . . trust no one to be your teacher nor your minister, except he be a man of God, walking in his ways and keeping his commandments. (Mosiah 23:14.)

A Servant to Others

I suppose the most difficult of all the qualities to acquire is that of humility, that quality of teachableness which allows us to change from what we are to something still better. This, I believe in a nutshell, is the secret to eternal progression. It's a great challenge to acquire this virtue relating to our educational endeavors and the learning process; it's an even greater challenge to acquire this quality and apply it to our eternal character development. Jesus, the greatest of all, phrased it this way:

> . . . Ye know that the princes of the Gentiles exercise dominion over them, and they that are great exercise authority upon them. But it shall not be so among you: but whosoever will be great among you, let him be your minister; And whosoever will be chief among you, let him be your servant: Even as the Son of man came not to be ministered unto, but to minister, and to give his life a ransom for many. (Matt. 20:25-28.)

As I understand the Master, he is saying that it is the natural tendency to think of a leader as one who should direct other's lives by telling them what to do, and then to accept the praise and recognition for being

He said that he was.

I then turned to Sister Emma, his wife, and said, "Sister Emma, are you trying to live your religion? Do you teach your children to obey their parents? Do you try to teach them to pray?"

To all these questions she answered, "Yes, I am trying to do so."

I then turned to Joseph and said, "I am now through with my questions as a teacher; and now if you have any instructions to give, I shall be happy to receive them."

He said, "God bless you, Brother William; and if you are humble and faithful, you shall have power to settle all difficulties that may come before you in the capacity of a teacher."

I then left my parting blessing upon him and his family, as a teacher, and took my departure.

—Juvenile Instructor, Vol. 27, p. 493.

wise enough to be supervisor to others. The concept held by Jesus was just the opposite. The man who works with God must think of himself as a servant; not one who is attended to by others, but one who attends to others in such a way as to provide for their needs. That this is one of the most interesting and exciting of all challenges is illustrated by this true story:

While teaching in one of our Institutes adjacent to a distinguished American university, I worked with a young man in our program that was one of the most self-centered fellows I've ever met. You know the kind —he had a great deal of "I" trouble. He played football at the university, and each day he came over to the Institute wearing his letterman's sweater and other insignia in such a way as to impress all whom he would meet. He was one of the most difficult students to reach I've ever known. Regardless of what I did, in or out of class, his only concern was of self and it was obvious that the only reason he came into the Institute program was for personal attention and adulation.

One afternoon, while at the Institute, I received a phone call from the hospital. It was a close friend calling. He wanted me to hurry down and assist him in administering to his newborn baby. In my haste to get to the floor of the hospital where the incubators were, I pushed a button that placed me on a different level. It was the children's ward. As I stepped into one of the rooms, it was one of the most gripping sights I've ever beheld. Every child hospitalized in that ward was entirely incapacitated and each lay helpless, completely dependent upon others. I got back on the elevator emotionally affected and hurried to my friend's side. After caring for the administration, I went back to the children's ward and talked to one of the nurses about the condition of her young patients and what might be done to help brighten their days. In the course of our

Every noble impulse; every unselfish expression of love; every brave suffering for the right; every surrender of self to something higher than self; every loyalty to an ideal; every unselfish devotion to principle; every helpfulness to humanity; every act of self-control; every fine courage of the soul, undefeated by pretense or policy, but by being, doing, and living of good for the very good's sake—that is spirituality.

The spiritual road has Christ as its ideal—not the gratification of the physical, for he that will save his life, yielding to that first gratification of a seeming need, will lose his life, lose his happiness, the pleasure of living at this present time. *If he would seek the real purpose of life, the individual must live for something higher than self.* He hears the Savior's voice, saying: "I am the way, the truth, and the life." (John 14:6.) Following that voice he soon learns that there is no one great thing which he can do to attain happiness or eternal life. He learns that "life is made up not of great sacrifices or duties, but of little things in which smiles and kindness and small obligations given habitually are what win and preserve the heart and secure comfort."

Spirituality, our true aim, is the consciousness of victory over self, and of communion with the Infinite. Spirituality impels one to conquer difficulties and acquire more and more strength. *To feel one's faculties unfolding, and truth expanding in the soul, is one of life's sublimest experiences.*

The man who sets his heart upon the things of the world, who does not hesitate to cheat his brother, who will lie for gain, who will steal from his neighbor, or, who, by slander, will rob another of his reputation, lives on a low, animal plane of existence, and either stifles his spirituality or permits it to lie dormant. To be thus carnally minded is to be spiritually dead.

conversation, she mentioned that one of the things people did to help the children was read to them occasionally. I asked what one had to do to be eligible for this service. "Just sign up on one of these cards," was the reply. I took one of the cards and signed up for an hour the following week, but in the place of my own name I wrote the name of my athletic friend. Now came the challenge of getting him there as scheduled.

The following week just before the appointed time, I telephoned my friend and said, with an element of surprise in my voice, "Bruce, *I need your help!* Will you help me?" "I gu-guess so," he replied, "but who is this?" "Your Institute teacher, Brother Dunn," I said. "I'll pick you up in 15 minutes in front of your place." "But, but——." By that time the phone on my end was back on the receiver.

At the appointed time, he was standing on the curb in front of his home, letterman's sweater and all. I opened the car door for him and said, "Hurry, get in." "What's so important?" he inquired. "I'll tell you on the way." He got in reluctantly and on the way to the hospital I told him I had signed him up to read some bedtime stories to a crippled girl for one hour. "Me—? Read to a crippled kid for one hour? Wait a minute!" By the time he had exhausted all his protests, we were at the hospital. "I'll meet you back here in one hour," I told him. "Look, I'm not going to read to any kid, take me back." I told him I wasn't going back that way for awhile—that I had several matters of business in another area. He finally got out of the car, and before he could say "no" again, I sped away from the scene, went around the block, and waited until it was time to pick him up.

As I approached the entrance to the hospital he was just coming out. He slowly got into the car. "How'd it go?" I asked. He put his head down and I

On the other hand, keeping in mind our daily vocations, the man who tills the soil, garners his fruit, increases his flocks and his herds, having in mind making better the world in which he lives, desiring to contribute to the happiness of his family and his fellows, and who does all things for the glory of God, will, to the extent that he denies himself for these ideals, develop his spirituality. Indeed, only to the extent that he does this will he rise above the plane of the animal world.

—David O. McKay, "Something Higher Than Self."

could see he had been greatly touched. Then he told me that he had been assigned to read to a little three-year-old girl who had never known a day out of bed. He went on to relate how embarrassed he was at first to read stories aloud to his little patient. But soon he forgot himself and became involved in doing all he could to help her. Then he told how deeply moved he was when his little friend asked him to lean down so she could kiss him goodby. "Brother Dunn," he said, "I hope you won't think I'm crazy but I signed up to read to those children for a whole month."

The boy was never the same again because he had had a glimpse into one of the Master's greatest teachings, "whosoever will lose his life for my sake shall find it." (Matt. 16:25.)

A certain family whom you are called to teach has become inactive in the Church to avoid responsibility. Which of the following best represents your honest attitude in caring for them?

1. Every person is a free agent. As such I feel it would be improper to impose my desires upon them. (See bottom of page.)

2. Sincere concern, proper example, and a desire to help them, will ultimately cause them to respond favorably. (Turn to page 43.)

Did you say, "Each person is a free agent. As such I feel it would be improper to impose my desires upon them"?

It is easy to understand such feelings. While I was in high school I chummed around with a non-Mormon friend. We have continued this relationship through the years. Never once in all those years did I take the opportunity to teach him about the Church and he never asked me. Since that time, however, he has become a very successful businessman.

While sitting in my office one day, I received a telephone call asking if I would go to lunch with him. While we were eating, he took occasion to test my sincerity concerning my job as Director of the Insitute of Religion. He wanted to know if I really enjoyed my work. I replied to him, "Tom, you know me well enough to know that I wouldn't be engaged in an assignment such as this unless I was sincerely commited to it." He responded, "That's what I thought. The reason I asked is that the other day I had two missionaries from your Church call at our home. We invited them in because they represented your faith and because we respect you. Would you like to know what we thought about it?" I told him I would. "Paul," he said, "without a doubt that is the greatest message I have ever heard. Thanks a lot for telling us about it!" Since that time I have been following the other alternative—maybe you should too. (Please return to page 41 and select the other alternative.)

Did you say, "Sincere concern, proper example, and a desire to help them, will ultimately cause them to respond favorably"?

This is usually the case. People find it difficult to resist an individual who is sincerely concerned over their spiritual welfare. One who will persist with kindness will find that the individuals will react in like manner. (Turn to page 45.)

About twenty years ago as a young soldier participating in the activity of this country during World War II, I found myself on the island of Okinawa, somewhere in my nineteenth year. In that serious mortal conflict, while trying to do what we could to preserve these freedoms, by chance I fell into the good graces of another young man who had fine ideals and high standards. Almost automatically we got together and shared the experiences of the war. Frequently we shared the same foxhole. One night during the month of May, our forces had sustained such heavy casualties that it became necessary for my friend and me to be separated. We were in different holes about fifty yards apart. It had commenced to rain about seven that evening, and it was a cold night. Along about eleven the enemy let go with a barrage that was almost unbelievable, and for almost two hours they harassed our lines with heavy artillery and mortar fire. Shortly after midnight one of these shells landed in the hole of my good friend. I could tell from the sound of the blast that it was serious. I called to him but couldn't get an answer, and the type of fighting we did in the Pacific prevented me from crawling over to offer aid. About an hour later I got a faint response indicating life still existed. All that night long, under heavy fire, I tried to call words of comfort to him, and finally as it commenced to get light I crawled to the hole of my friend and found that he had almost become submerged in the water from the heavy rain of the night before.

As I lifted him out on that cold, muddy bank and laid his head in my lap, I tried to offer what physical comfort I could under those conditions, wiping his brow and face with a handkerchief. He was almost limp with death now. I said, "Harold, you hold on, and I'll get you to the aid station just as soon as I can. It's only a few hundred yards away." "No," he said, "I know

How You can Establish a Right Relationship with God in terms of Dedication to His Kingdom

It is my conviction that ultimately all men must decide for themselves what and whom they will serve. A person's dominant ambition and aspiration is a true index of the god whom he is presently serving. One may choose power, wealth, love, position, or family. Only one alternative is given however, to the man who would work with God.

> No man can serve two masters: for either he will hate the one, and love the other; or else he will hold to the one, and despise the other. Ye cannot serve God and mammon. (Matt. 6:24.)

It is a clinically validated truth that an individual who attempts to lead two lives, serving his own interests on the one hand, and then attempting to serve the interests of others, soon develops what is termed a "split personality" or schizophrenia. The Apostle James wrote about this "spiritual schizophrenia" after observing the attempt of some Christians in his day to lead this double life. He summed it up this way, "A double minded man is unstable in all his ways." (James 1:8.) In other words, the consequences of trying to serve both God and man lead to insecurity and instability.

For the man who would work with God, the only way out of this dilemna is to heed the counsel of the One whom the Father sent to instruct us. He said:

> . . . If any man will come after me, let him deny himself, and take up his cross, and follow me. (Matt. 16:24.)

> Lay not up for yourselves treasures upon earth,

this is the end, and I've held on as long as possible because I want you to do two things for me, Paul, if you would." I said, "You just name it, Harold." He said, "If you are permitted to live through this terrible ordeal, will you somehow get word to my parents and tell them how grateful I am for their teaching and influence which has enabled me to meet death with security and calmness, and this in turn will help sustain them." (And I'm happy to report to you I was able to fulfill that commitment.)

"Second, Paul," he said, "if you ever have the opportunity to talk to the youth of the world, will you tell them for me that it is a sacred privilege to lay down my life for the principles that we have been defending here today." And with that testimony on his lips he, like so many others before, gave his life for the principles of freedom and righteousness.

Well, as we buried Harold along with his comrades, close friends, and associates, we placed over a cemetery on Okinawa this inscription, and I think it still stands for all to observe who would, *"We gave our todays in order that you might have your tomorrows."*

> where moth and rust doth corrupt. . . . But lay up for yourselves treasures in heaven, where neither moth nor rust doth currupt. . . . For where your treasure is, there will your heart be also. (Matt. 6: 19-21.)

> But seek ye first the kingdom of God, and his righteousness; and all these things shall be added unto you. (Matt. 6:33.)

To be a participant in the building of his kingdom, a whole-souled dedication is required. Such dedication is characterized by serving the Church with "all your heart, might, mind, and strength." Thus when a call comes to serve, whatever it may be, the man who works with God can answer, ". . . as for me and my house, we will serve the Lord." (Josh. 24:15.)

Which of the following represents best the attitude you bring into your present church assignment?

1. Of all responsibilities, I regard my calling in the Church as the most important because of the opportunity to dedicate my life to the kingdom of God. (See bottom of page.)
2. I feel that a person should accept a church assignment, but there are other things such as one's work, or other interests, that are equally important to his progress. (Turn to page 49.)

Did you say, "Of all responsibilities, I regard my calling in Church as the most important because of the opportunity to dedicate my life to the kingdom of God"?

This was a tough choice because your natural inclination would be to consider your own family first. You were quite correct in this feeling. One's family is the most important consideration of all the work in the Lord's kingdom. As President McKay has said, "No suc-

cess in life (or in the Church) can compensate for failure in the home." (Turn to page 45.)

Did you say, "I feel that a person should accept a church assignment, but there are other things such as one's work, or other interests, that are equally important to his progress"?

Perhaps an alternative such as this was unfair because you thought of commitments to your family and loved ones. And certainly this is the MOST IMPORTANT aspect of the Lord's program. On the other hand, if you consider your interests outside the home equal to your church responsibility, it might be well to examine these values in the light of your eternal future. Most of us have a tendency to forget the long-term goals as we favor our mortal interests. (Turn to page 55.)

CHAPTER 1 SELF-TEST

To obtain the maximum benefit from this chapter, take a pencil and paper and complete the following exercise:

1. Explain in writing how you can improve in your own relationship with God in terms of the salvation of your own soul. (Page 15.)
2. Briefly explain what you can do to improve your relationship with God by caring for your fellow men. (Page 27.)
3. How can you improve your dedication to his kingdom? (Page 45.)

Chapter 2

THE MAN WHO CAN RIGHTEOUSLY INFLUENCE OTHERS

At the end of this chapter you should be able to:

1. SPECIFY WHAT THINGS YOU CAN IMPROVE UPON IN GETTING OTHERS TO FOLLOW YOUR LEADERSHIP.

2. STATE THE SPECIFIC THINGS YOU CAN DO NOW TO IMPROVE THE MORALE IN YOUR ORGANIZATION.

3. INDICATE HOW YOU CAN CORRECT ANOTHER PERSON WITHOUT AFFECTING YOUR RELATIONSHIP.

Chapter 2

THE MAN WHO CAN RIGHTEOUSLY INFLUENCE OTHERS

How to Influence Others to Follow your Lead

There is only one real challenge in leadership: To righteously influence others to follow willingly. There are many reasons why people are not willing to follow a leader, but two of the most common problems seem to be:

1. The leader is insincere or insecure in his leadership assignment.
2. The leader attempts to manipulate and control others. The Prophet Joseph Smith said, "We have learned by sad experience that it is the nature and disposition of almost all men, as soon as they get a little authority, as they suppose, they will immediately begin to exercise unrighteous dominion. (D. & C. 121:39.)

The treatment of this book is dedicated to help you solve the first problem. It is hoped this chapter will assist you in solving the second.

Continuing with that great "human relations" revelation, the Lord sets down the pattern by which all

THE THREE C'S OF LEADERSHIP

To be a real leader, a person must observe what I call the "three C's of Leadership."

First, he will make as many problems as possible a matter of *common council.* People will always cooperate in carrying out a policy if they feel they have had a voice in making it. "Our plan" is always better than "my plan."

The next C is *courteous consideration.* More than a ready smile and convenient politeness, courteous consideration is the willingness of an executive to give of his personal time when it is not convenient. It is his capacity to give an understanding and patient hearing to the ideas of subordinates, and to offer encouragement and counsel when it is needed—not just when it is easy to give.

The final C is to *concede credit.* Nothing costs an executive so little and nothing can provide greater pleasure or bring closer cooperation than to give the other fellow credit for something he has done well.

—H. W. Pristis, Jr.

priesthood leaders should attempt to influence others. Let's review it.

> No power or *influence* can or ought to be maintained by virtue of the priesthood, only by persuasion, by long-suffering, by gentleness and meekness, and by love unfeigned; By kindness, and pure knowledge, which shall greatly enlarge the soul without hypocrisy, and without guile. (D. & C. 121:41-43.)

There would be few, if any, who don't believe in these remarkable virtues. Putting them into practice is something again. Perhaps it will be helpful to consider how effective and influential leaders have put into practice these principles and proved this very terse statement to be the most effective formula for righteously influencing others.

1. *Persuasion*—This principle consists of inducing another person to action on belief. It is the opposite of ordering or compelling another. To illustrate: One priesthood leader was having a difficult time getting a certain home teacher to do his assigned responsibility. He called him into an oral evaluation, listened to his problems, and then calmly explained how five families were being totally "cut off" from any communication from the bishop when he didn't do his task. He then told the brother that if he didn't want to do his assignment, they could call another, but they preferred him. The home teacher responded positively to this approach and has since greatly improved his work.

2. *Long-suffering*—This principle implies that a leader will use patience with his workers when they do inferior work. It is opposite to impatience and ridicule. A bishop recently explained how he wanted to release a certain worker because of the job she was doing. He finally called her in, talked with her, and found that she had no knowledge that her area of failure was a

The only responsibility that a man cannot evade in this life is the one he thinks of least, his personal influence. Man's conscious influence, when he is on dress parade, when he is posing to impress those around him, is woefully small. But his unconscious influence, the silent, subtle radiation of his personality, the effect of his words and acts, the trifles he never considers, is tremendous. Every moment of life he is changing, to a degree, the life of the whole world. Every man has an atmosphere which is affecting every other. So silent and unconsciously is this influence working, that man may forget that it exists.

Into the hands of every individual is given a marvelous power for good or for evil, the silent, unconscious, unseen influence of his life. This is simply the constant radiation of what a man really is, not what he pretends to be. Every man, by his mere living, is radiating sympathy, or sorrow, or morbidness, or cynicism, or happiness, or hope, or any of a hundred other qualities. Life is a state of constant radiation and absorption; to exist is to radiate; to exist is to be the recipient of radiations.

—William George Jordan, *The Majesty of Calmness,* (New Jersey: Fleming H. Revell Company), pp. 19-20. Used by permission of Fleming H. Revell Company.

part of her responsibility. Upon learning what she could do and how, the entire situation changed and her appreciation for the bishop increased.

3. *Gentleness*—The English clergyman, James Hamilton, has said that "true gentleness is love in society, holding intercourse with those around it. It is considerateness; it is tenderness of feelings . . . it is love in all depths." One church leader always takes the opportunity to pen a small note of thanks or letter of congratulations to those in the ward who render a service. A teacher always calls her students on the phone when they have made some contribution in the way of speaking or performance in the ward.

4. *Meekness*—This is the quality of being teachable and open-minded. When we raise our hands in sustaining approval of the church leadership, it is a covenant to submit to their direction and counsel. The meek are those who are willing to grow, who through their democratic spirit are able to win the love and appreciation of others and who with repentant spirits are anxious for God's direction and help. One of our great leaders continually seeks the Lord's help to sustain him in his weakness. He attributes all his success and ability to his submission completely to the Lord.

5. *Love unfeigned*—Most react unfavorably to an insincere "human relations" approach. We sense that the person is not being authentic. Unfeigned love is charity with a concern. It says this to the other person, "I really care how you feel. I'm concerned that you feel the way you do. What may I do to help?" Hawthorne said, "No man can, for any considerable time, wear one face to himself, and another to the multitude, without finally getting bewildered as to which is the true one."

6. *Kindness*—This is the quality of treating people

An Ancient Egyptian said: (Ptah—Hotep)

If you are in a position of one to whom petitions are made, be courteous and listen to the petitioner's story. Do not stop his words until he has poured out all that is in his heart and has said all that he came to say. A man with a grievance loves the official who will accept what he states and let him talk out his troubles fully. A kind word will illuminate his heart, but if an official stops the flow of words people will say, "Why should that fellow have the power to behave this way?"

with respect. Its counterpart is indifference and brusqueness. There are a few leaders who feel that the administration of their job is more important than the people who come to them for help. When disrupted in what they may be doing, they convey unconcern by brusqueness or aloofness. In contrast, one of the most influential bishops who owns his own business will not talk to any of his members till he can give them his individual attention. There are moments when he can't be interrupted so he tells them this: "I feel I owe it to you as a friend to give you my individual attention. I can't do that at this moment. Would you return at a time when we can talk uninterrupted?" Emerson understood this to be one's greatest gift when he said, "Rings and jewels are not gifts, but apologies for gifts. The only gift is a portion of thyself."

Kindness, however, is more than waiting till someone comes and asks for help. One Sunday School teacher looks for many ways she can go out of her way to do little things for class members. If you're lacking for any of these ideas, pick up the little book, *Try Giving Yourself Away* by David Dunn, Prentice-Hall Incorporated. (Incidentally, he's not a relative.)

What all these virtues add up to, in a word, is "charity" toward all men. There seem to be two requirements for obtaining this quality of the heart which will cause that one's "confidence will wax strong in the presence of God," and that others will follow him willingly.

1. One must realize that charity is not inborn. It is a gift of God. The Prophet Mormon counseled that this gift only comes through earnest prayer.

> Wherefore, my beloved brethren, pray unto the Father with all the energy of heart, *that ye may be filled with this love,* which he hath bestowed upon

There are at least three kinds of communication: (a) informative, (b) persuasive, (c) entertaining.

Although we must recognize that the distinction between the three major types of communication is not hard and fast, it is nevertheless an important one, because it is a distinction involving the central, guiding purpose of the communication. The purpose of informative communication is stated in terms of the amount and kinds of information to be included; of persuasive communication, in terms of the beliefs or opinions to be changed or formed; and of entertaining communication, in terms of the desired pleasurable responses. Thus the distinction in purpose is a very real one. If you know exactly what the purpose of your communication is, it will serve as a guide for your preparation—a reminder that each bit of informative, persuasive, or entertaining material that you include should contribute something to the accomplishment of that purpose.

—Howard H. Dean, *Effective Communication* (New York: Prentice-Hall, Inc., 1955), pp. 14-15. Used by permission.

all who are true followers of his Son, Jesus Christ; that ye may become the sons of God; that when he shall appear we shall be like him, for we shall see him as he is; that we may have this hope; that we may be purified as he is pure. (Moro. 7:48.)

2. One must be willing to "lose himself" in the interest of others. In other words, we must be willing to serve with the end in view of being a servant, not the master.

How to Improve the Morale in an Organization

Over the past 25 years, I've had the privilege of being associated with a number of organizations. These were the army, professional baseball, a grocery chain, and the Institute program of the Church. What would you guess was the factor common to all that most contributed to the success of each organization? Not knowledge, talent or experience—important as these things are. It was morale. The army called it *"espirit de corps."* Baseball called it "team spirit." The grocery chain termed it "cooperation." And the Institute program calls it "brotherhood." It all adds up to the one indispensable factor to success or winning—*Morale.* What creates good morale?

1. Effective communication must be established among your organizational members. When communication "breaks down" in an organization the morale goes with it. How do you develop it? Communication is a two-way street. You know you have effective communication when those with whom you work can say what they feel without feeling their job is in jeopardy. Because most of us have a tendency to defend our decisions or actions, this is sometimes difficult. For example, an organizational leader in the Church, who is extremely

The Colonel Told the Major—At nine o'clock tomorrow there will be an eclipse of the sun, something which does not occur every day. Get the men to fall out in the company street in their fatigues so that they will see this rare phenomenon, and I will explain it to them. In case of rain, we will not be able to see anything, so take the men to the gym.

The Major Told the Captain—By order of the Colonel, tomorrow at nine o'clock there will be an eclipse of the sun. If it rains you will not be able to see it from the company street, so then, in fatigues, the eclipse of the sun will take place in the gym, something that does not occur every day.

The Captain Told the Lieutenant—By order of the Colonel in fatigues tomorrow at nine o'clock in the morning the inauguration of the eclipse of the sun will take place in the gym. The Colonel will give the order if it should rain, something which occurs every day.

The Lieutenant Told the Sergeant—Tomorrow at nine the Colonel in fatigues will eclipse the sun in the gym, as it occurs every day if it is a nice day. If it rains, then in the company street.

The Sergeant Told the Corporal—Tomorrow at nine the eclipse of the Colonel in Fatigues will take place by cause of the sun. If it rains in the gym, something which does not take place every day, you will fall out in the company street.

This Is What the Privates Understood—Tomorrow, if it rains, it looks as if the sun will eclipse the Colonel in the gym. It is a shame that this does not occur every day.

Don't be blind to people.

capable, asks his subordinates for suggestions on how to improve the organization. When one suggests a matter that needs improving, the leader's immediate reaction is to defend what has been. As a result, he has cut himself off from future evaluation. His line of cummunication is broken. His fellow workers know that what he wants is not new ideas or suggestions for improving but an endorsement of what is now being done. His subordinates tell him exactly what he wants to hear, not what he should hear and as a result morale is lessened and the organization effected. The best way to insure good communication is to build what William Dyer calls the "climate of trust." This is developed through the following steps:

a. Express your sincere interest to the organizational members that you want their honest feelings. Be completely "open" and above-board. What is said should in no way affect the future standing of the person making the suggestions or giving the criticism.

b. When members give this "feedback," don't evaluate or defend your position, just listen.

It's easy to commend an outstanding worker in a church organization, but what has amazed me in assignments about the Church is the remarkable tolerance for mediocrity or poor performance. "You can't tell a person they're doing a poor job, can you?" is the question I frequently hear when areas of deficiency are discussed. My answer to that question is: "That depends on whether you have explained the expectations of satisfactory performance when he was called. If you haven't, then he deserves to know. If you have, and committed him to that performance level, it's a simple matter to say, 'Ted, you'll recall when you were called to this assignment, *we agreed* upon a certain minimum performance to get the job done effectively. Do you feel that the performance of your job has met the standard *we agreed* upon? If not what can you and I do to improve it?' " Perhaps it's necessary to review the assignment. In most cases, the performance will improve immediately, or alternatives could be suggested.

c. Provide the organization with all the pertinent facts bearing on the situation. Don't presume they know everything. Keep them well informed.

d. Let all who are affected by a decision have a "voice" in making the decision.

2. Each person in the organization must know his purpose and place. Too many are called to assignments without an adequate understanding of what they are supposed to do and how they fit in. A good way to test the morale of your organization in this area is to ask yourself, "How many people have asked to be released in the last six months?" Oh yes, they resign graciously. They haven't got the time! The husband's working hours have changed! (Now this doesn't mean that all people who resign don't have legitimate reasons.) Constant turnover, however, is a sign of dissatisfied, insecure individuals. In a "climate of trust" they often tell their real reason which might include: "I don't like my job. It's not important enough for me," or "I'm not secure in my assignment. I don't know how to do it," or "I'm not certain what's expected of me."

One effective church leader after calling a person to a position explains the new job or task to the individual so that he understands its purpose and how the job relates to the total organization. The leader then carefully explains to the person what is expected of him and how his part and contribution affects the whole. His next step is to show the person how to *do* the job or assign some competent individual to do the training. He then sees to it that the mistakes, if any, are corrected while the person is in the training process. He then allows the person to function in his assignment, checking with him to determine periodically his feelings toward the assignment. The rule this leader follows is: "It's not enough to give a member of the Church a job and leave

"Individual value is the basis of democracy; individual affirmation is its process; and individual responsibility is its motive force."

—Mary P. Follett

him to it. You've got to ensure he gets a successful experience in the performance of that job."

3. Every worker deserves to know where he stands. It has been said, "If you really want to insult a man, to show a man how unimportant he really is—ignore him!" It's a fact that if a person is not sincerely apprised of his contribution to the organization, his work will be adversely affected. As an example, research workers have found that the morale factors most closely related to high production are these:

a. Immediate supervision—the workers expect the supervisor to be a liaison between them and the organization.

b. Satisfaction with job.

c. Compatibility with fellow workers.

d. Satisfaction with the organizational purpose—they felt, in other words, that they were making a worthwhile contribution.

e. Reasonable rewards—applied to church work, this would be honest appreciation and commendation and a measurable result in program growth.

f. General physical and mental health.

4. Every person responds favorably to small attentions. The effective leader who can work with people doesn't wait for the person to come to him before he gives small attentions. He goes to them. It is comparable to a courting process before marriage. The leader shows his interest by the little things he does that mean so much, but not in an effort to manipulate or control. Sincere expression is the key.

How would you handle this problem of morale?

In one of the organizations of a ward, much difficulty was being experienced in getting the young people to participate. The bishop asked a number of them why they didn't show more interest. The kids replied, "We always have to do what they (the leaders) want to do, and we never get what we want to do." "What do you want to do?" asked the bishop. "We want to have some dances and parties!" "Aren't you having dances and parties now?" "No," they replied. The bishop then took the matter up at the ward council meeting. He told the ward leadership of the desires of the young people. The reply he received from the ward leaders directly involved with the youth program was, "We know what the kids want, but every time we try something like that, it gets out of hand." "What do you mean?" asked the bishop. "Well, if we schedule a dance, pretty soon some of our young people start to do some of the new dances that don't fit the occasion. So to prevent this happening, we have just stopped the dances altogether."

Which of the following best indicates how to improve the problem of morale among these young people:

1. Bring the young people together in a group and tell them that the standard has been set by the Church and they should be willing to have dances that would conform to the standard. (See bottom of page.)

2. Call a group of young people together with the youth leaders and discuss the reasons for the policy. In addition let them indicate how their desires could be satisfied within the limits of church standards. (Turn to page 73.)

Did you say you would "bring the young people together in a group and tell them that the standard has

been set by the Church and they should be willing to have dances that would conform to the standard"?

This is one way to handle the problem, but would it improve the morale of the young people? Let's consider why the young people might react negatively to the "telling" approach.

1. They have had no opportunity to express their feelings.
2. They hadn't been adequately informed as to the reason for the dance standard.
3. They hadn't had an opportunity to help in planning activities which would be in accordance with church standards.

By this approach, a policy will have been dictated, but the morale problem will probably remain. (Turn to page 71 and select the other alternative.)

Did you say you would "call a group of young people together with the youth leaders and discuss the reasons for the policy"?

This answer is exactly what the wise bishop did. He could see that his organizational leaders were too concerned about program needs—keeping the young people under control.

The bishop suggested that the leaders meet with a committee of young people to determine how the desires of the young people could be satisfied within the limits of church standards. This was done. At the first meeting, the bishop came in and explained to the young people on the committee that the Church had no

THE LEADER'S KIT

A real leader has the ability to get others to work willingly through his influence and example. His efforts are directed toward influencing people to want to do certain things—not to make them obey his commands.

Instruct Clearly—Speak clearly and simply so as to be thoroughly understood.

Lead—don't Drive—You must not drive but you can create drive in your group.

Play Fair—Those who work with you must respect you —there can be no respect if you do not play fair.

Display A Friendly Attitude—A friendly attitude begets understanding and cooperation.

Appreciate Honest Effort—If effort is misdirected, it may be because you have not instructed properly. Give credit for honest effort, not results alone.

Keep Your Promises—You gain respect and greater cooperation by keeping your promises. Do not promise unless you are sure you can deliver.

Keep An Open Mind—Be willing to listen and learn.

Be Loyal to Those Above and Below—The Lord has called each of us. Those in leadership need your dedication and respect.

Be Considerate of Everyone—You don't have to be soft to be considerate, but being considerate is a warm, human trait, and it will win cooperation from everyone for you.

Be Consistent in All Things—Inconsistency creates misunderstandings, ill will and distrust.

—Author Unknown

intent of depriving them of having fun. "The fact is," said the bishop, "we want you to have fun. But we also know that when young people go out on a dance floor and display bodily movements the way some do, it sets in motion the biological processes which motivate both boy and girl. It also places emphasis upon the physical rather than the spiritual which can lead to complication. It's not what happens so much on the dance floor as what often happens *after* the dance is over. That is what we try to prevent." The reaction to this explanation by the bishop was received most favorably by the young people. One girl said, "Why didn't you tell us that in the first place! We just thought you didn't want us to have fun."

From several meetings like this, a wholesome activity program was worked out that satisfied the desires of the young people within the propriety of church standards. The result was a participation of the youth that far exceeded the expectations of their leaders.

How to Correct Another Person

There will be times when it is necessary to correct a person working under your direction. Actually, a person wants to know and deserves to know where he stands in relation to his job performance. Let's illustrate three ways of correcting others without effecting your relationship with them:

1. Commend the person when he does a job right. This is a positive rather than a negative approach in correcting people. This approach came to my attention while traveling among the stakes. A high councilman reported that a branch president who had been noted for his lengthy announcements had taken only a moment to make them that Sunday, and he had done it in

'Tis the human touch in the world that counts,
The touch of your hand in mine,
Which means far more to the fainting heart
Than shelter and bread and wine;
For shelter is gone when the night is o'er
And bread lasts only a day,
But the touch of the hand and the sound of the voice
Sing on in the soul always.

—Spencer Michael Free

such a way as not to detract from the sacred occasion. "Did you commend him for doing it right?" asked the stake president. "Be sure you do so the next time you see him." This principle is a sound one. People feel good about improving when they are given sincere approval.

2. Commend the person for sincere efforts, but indicate where and how he can improve if need be.

One stake president's practice is to assign a problem area to one of the brethren on the high council to study, evaluate, gather all the facts, and then come back with a recommendation. When the high councilman reports back, the president allows him to explain the modifications or recommendations in full. He always commends him for his efforts by expressing as only he can, the sincere appreciation for what he has done. The stake presidency then give the recommendations their prayerful consideration. If the recommendations meet with approval, the president again reports to the council that Brother______'s study has been most helpful in implementing the program as follows. On other occasions he may report back to the high councilman with this observation: Brother_____, we appreciate your

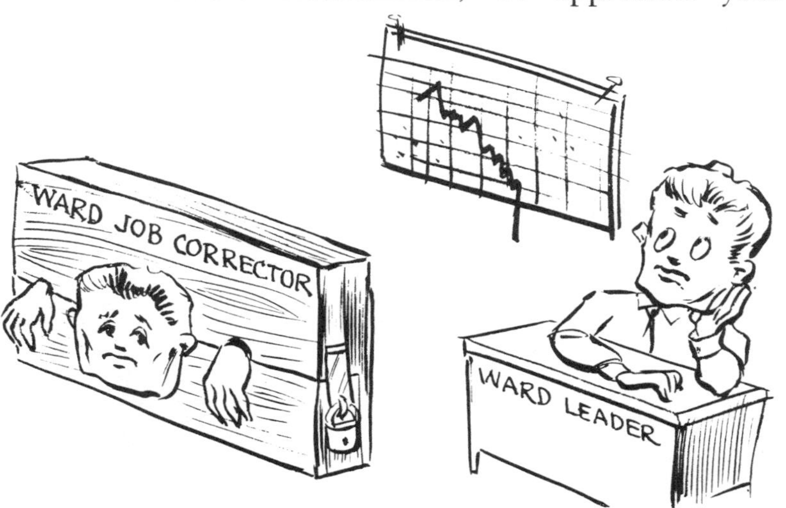

"There are really only two ways by which the individual may be controlled. Either he must be controlled by someone else, or he must govern himself. He may govern himself by seeking only his own immediate good, without regard for others, or even to their conscious and deliberate detriment. Or he may govern himself through common agreement with others, and in the light of his own and their needs and purposes."

—Earl C. Kelly

efforts, but the findings are not as conclusive as we would like or need. Please take it back and look it over again and give us a more complete report in two weeks. We hope you know how much we appreciate what you have done and your thoroughness to this point.

A home teaching secretary takes time each month in the priesthood executive meeting to call attention, with attractive charts, to the places where the home teachers may improve. He further brings into meetings mimeographed reminders of areas wherein the individual teachers can improve.

A bishop uses this approach: He calls in a leader and asks, "If you were to improve on your program in any way, what would you do?" He then commits him to his own suggestions.

3. "Reproving betimes with sharpness when moved upon by the Holy Ghost; and then showing forth afterwards an increase of love toward him whom thou hast reproved." (D. & C. 121:43.)

An effective elders quorum president demonstrates what I believe to be the proper application of this principle. On one occasion he called for a report to be given at an executive meeting. He had previously committed one of his brethren to accomplish an assignment and to be ready to report at the meeting. Well in advance of the meeting he reminded him of the date, time and place and what was expected of him. He then had it entered as an item on the agendum, a copy of which was sent to this quorum member. At the designated date and hour, the elder reported he was not prepared. The president replied in the most kind and gentle manner I have heard, "But Brother______, we were counting on you to give us this report. A great deal depended upon your report and recommendations. The entire quorum project will be delayed now." Then

We cannot repeat the point too often—the person who shows no judgment of human nature will be a failure as a leader. In reproving, like all things, there is more than one way. A shoe salesman told a woman trying on pumps, "Madam, one of your feet is larger than the other."

She went off in a huff.

In the next shoeshop the salesman said, "Madam, one of your feet is smaller than the other."

And she bought.

he turned to another brother and asked him to prepare a similar report and to be ready to present it in two weeks. I watched with interest the reaction of the delinquent elder. He was at first ashamed, but then the president expressed his appreciation for what this brother had done *in other ways.* Before the meeting closed he asked his chastised associate to remain. When they were alone (I later learned), he told him, "I want you to know how much we appreciate you and your service. You have much to offer and I want you to know it's a pleasure to have you among us." The brother ended up apologizing for letting the president and quorum down and committed himself to greater dedication.

You will recognize that this president's approach couldn't be used with all people in all situations. Timing, inspiration, and love are the factors that make the principle work.

Two things need to be remembered if reproving is found necessary: (1) It should never be done in anger, and (2) it should be done to help the individual improve —in other words, to satisfy a higher need.

Brother C. was a ward leader working with the young boys. The boys thought he was tremendous! He showed his interest in them by frequently taking them for hikes, outings, or boating trips. On Sunday mornings, however, he had extreme difficulty getting to his meetings because of sleeping in, and when he did come, he was never prepared with a lesson. He was one of the few men in the ward to whom the boys responded.

In your opinion, the best way to improve this situation would be to:

1. Release him if he doesn't show more responsibility. (Turn to page 83.)
2. Call him in and commend him for the way he is able to influence the boys. Then ask him how

his assignment can be improved. (See bottom of page.)

3. Let the situation go on and hope that it will eventually improve. (Turn to page 85.)

Did you say, "Release him if he doesn't show more responsibility"?

This would probably solve your problem for the Sunday meetings, but replacing him in the boys' eyes would be difficult since he does an effective job in meeting their needs out of class. And if released, he would not be in a position to grow and develop as he could with some directional guidance. Let's consider another alternative. (Turn to page 81.)

Did you say, "Let the situation go and hope it will eventually improve"? All the waiting in the world won't improve the situation.

I would agree that you would probably have a difficult time in finding a better "boys man," but this brother deserves to know that his standard of performance in the class is not acceptable. Let's suppose that you were in his position. You love to work with the boys, but don't feel good about your accomplishments in class. Wouldn't you want some help? Let's reconsider another alternative. (Return to page 81 and select another answer.)

Did you say you would "call him in and commend him for the way he is able to influence the boys and then ask him how his assignment can be improved"?

I agree! You have recognized his ability to win the boys' respect and admiration. By soliciting his suggestions for improvement, it will probably not be necessary for you to bring the problem up since he won't be totally satisfied with his performance. When the problem is brought out, possible solutions could be discussed. One method of committing him to a minimum acceptable standard of performance would be the following:

> "Again I want to thank you for all you do, Brother C. Please know you have the appreciation of every mother and father in the ward. We've never had a more effective worker and leader of youth. Now, you say you could even improve on what you're doing by preparing your lessons and coming on time to your meetings. Do you really mean that?" "Yes." "Is there any way we can assist you?" "If there is I'll let you know." "Will you do it then?" "Yes, I will." "We believe you're a man of your word and when you say you'll do it, we believe it will be done."

How would you handle this one? A talented and sensitive sister lives in your ward. She has caused a great deal of "bad" feelings because of gossip. Which of the following would represent the best way to handle this problem:

1. Tell those who have been "hurt" by her to ignore the problem explaining that this is just her personality. (Turn to page 87.)

2. Call the sister in and tell her how much she is appreciated in the ward, then frankly explain to her the problem and feelings she has caused. (Turn to page 87.)

Did you say you would "call her in and tell her how much she is appreciated in the ward; then frankly explain to her the problem and feelings she has caused"?

This has been found to be the far more successful approach for the reason that you are giving her the dignity and respect of a private disclosure of her problem, and what it has done to affect others. She can then be guided into resolving this difficulty by apologizing herself to those whom she has offended.

Did you say you would "tell those who have been 'hurt,' to ignore the problem explaining that this is just her personality"?

Let's consider the implications of this approach. You would explain to the people that had been offended by her remarks that this was just her way of doing things and after all with such a personality what can you expect. They in turn would tell others what you said, and then the sister would become hurt and offended. Then you . . . Well, I think you can see where this approach might cause more serious problems than it would solve. (Please return to page 85 and select the other alternative.)

CHAPTER 2 SELF-TEST

1. In Section 121 of the Doctrine and Covenants, there are a number of virtues that are desirable in righteous leadership. How does a person attain these? Specify on a separate sheet of paper the things you can do to improve upon in getting others to follow your direction. (Page 57.)
2. What do you consider to be the most important morale factor to a church organization? What can you start doing now to improve the morale in your organization? (Page 63.)
3. There were three ways suggested in which you could correct another and get him to like you for it. What were they? Which one could you start to use now that would improve your relationship with those with whom you work? (Page 75.)

Chapter 3

THE MAN WHO CAN WORK EFFECTIVELY WITH PEOPLE

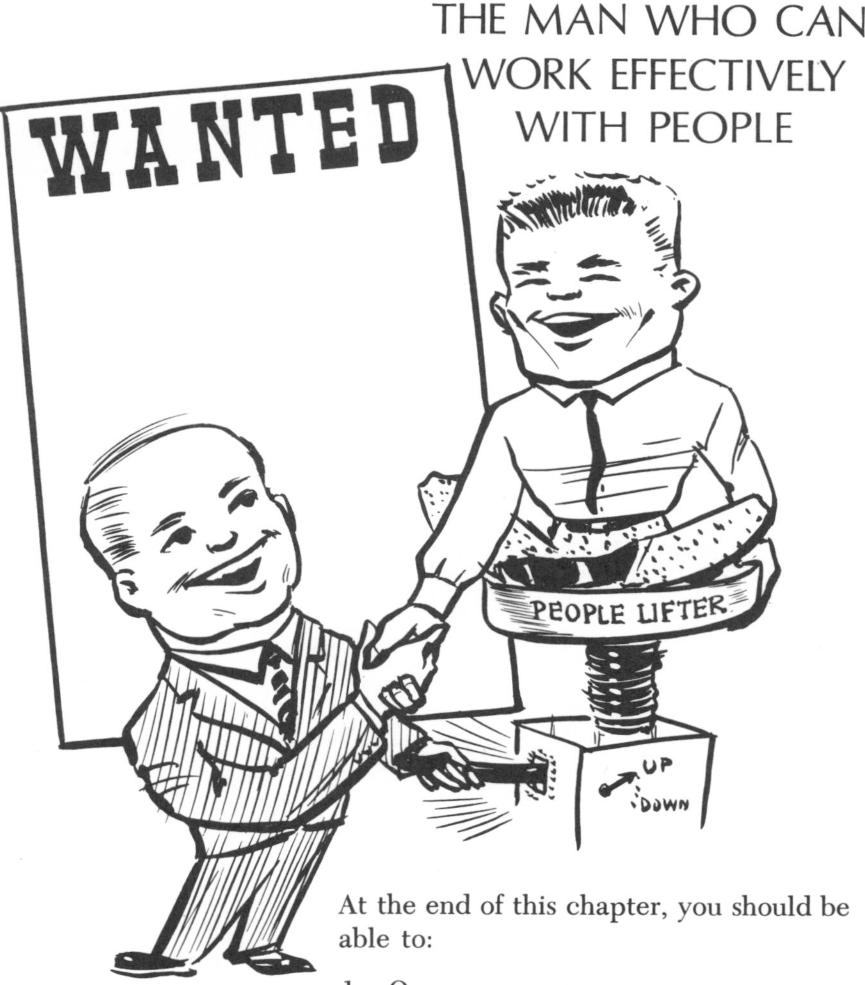

At the end of this chapter, you should be able to:

1. Outline the steps you would follow in overcoming fear.
2. State the reason why people behave the way they do.
3. Explain how you can most effectively meet the needs of the individuals with whom you work.

Chapter 3

THE MAN WHO CAN WORK EFFECTIVELY WITH PEOPLE

Know Thyself

Many years ago, a wise Athenian said, "Know thyself." Socrates had observed and understood that the man who is most capable as a leader of others is one who understands his capacity and limitations. So before we turn our attention to working effectively with others in a leadership capacity, we should give consideration to an honest appraisal of ourselves.

Making this honest appraisal of yourself will be difficult. It will require that you seek insight from the divine source. In addition one needs to be willing to listen and to accept honest evaluation from those who know him best. We all want to be what we think we should be. All of us fall short of the ideal. To maintain an image of worth, many of us have succumbed to the temptation of pretending to be NOW what we consider our ideal. The prophets warn that pretense is one of the adversary's greatest tools because it prohibits a person with divine capacity from achieving his ultimate potential. Often as we endeavor to protect our self-image we impede our progress by resorting to some of the following defenses:

1. We tend to avoid situations in which we antici-

TRIED AND TRUE ADVICE FOR A YOUNG EXECUTIVE

Don't be afraid to make mistakes. If you risk little, you will probably win little. Welcome ideas from your employees. Good ideas from the rank and file are a credit to you as well as to the originator and no executive worth his salt ever feels threatened by a good idea, whatever its source. Always keep your promises. And don't make promises you can't keep. Never underestimate your fellow man. Good ideas can come from humble sources. Fertile minds are not always labeled with a college degree. Learn to use "horse sense" in dealing with others. In other words, learn to treat others as you would like to be treated. Keep in touch with key members of your department. Don't shut yourself up in an "ivory tower" and don't depend upon assistants to do all your leg-work for you. In controversial matters, especially, get the story yourself. Delegate responsibility to subordinates. By doing so, you do three things: You ease your own work load; you train deserving workers for more important posts; and you groom a competent successor who is ready to step into your shoes when it's time for you to move up the ladder or when retirement comes.

—C. G. Scholtz

pate failure. The Sunday School teacher may have a discipline problem in class which indicates to her that she is a failure, so she resigns with an acceptable explanation, such as "My husband needs me at home." A home teacher fears to visit his inactive families because of his feeling of insecurity in helping them so he reports to his priesthood leader, "They don't want the home teachers anymore." Some people, because of this fear of failure, become inactive themselves rather than accept resonsibility.

2. We alibi our failures. The church worker, instead of admitting lack of commitment to his assignment may report, "I don't have the time during the week to do all that's required." A husband displays a temper around his children and excuses himself by saying, "Even the Lord uses righteous indignation!" The housewife feels insecure around her non-Latter-day Saint friends so she justifies her feelings, "I don't have anything in common with my neighbors."

3. We blame others or conditions for our failures. An auxiliary teacher had to be released because he wasn't doing his job so he criticizes, "The bishop didn't give me the support I needed in the class." The critical member may say, "It's no wonder that this ward doesn't get anywhere the way the leaders are directing the program." "I would be more active," says another, "if there were more members who lived their religion."

How to Overcome Fear of Failure

We must first recognize our own shortcomings and then we are in a position to do something about them. Shortcomings are best overcome by recognizing our strengths. Here are some suggestions:

And if men come unto me I will show unto them their weakness. I give unto men weakness that they may be humble; and my grace is sufficient for all men that humble themselves before me; for if they humble themselves before me, and have faith in me, then will I make weak things become strong unto them.

(Ether 12:27.)

Do not pray for easy lives—pray to be stronger men. Do not pray for tasks equal to your powers—pray for powers equal to your tasks.

The superior man will watch over himself when he is alone. He examines his heart that there may be nothing wrong there and that he may have no cause of dissatisfaction within himself.

1. Realize that you have a limitless potential which you will never reach in this life. As a child of God, you have all it takes to achieve your goals and aspirations. In order to discover your strengths four things are required:

a. Seek divine help in seeing yourself as you really are. (Ether 12:27.)

b. Have those who know you best give an honest evaluation.

c. Make a careful self-analysis. Write on a sheet of paper all of the strengths as well as the limitations that you see in yourself.

d. Having found your strengths it is necessary to consciously apply them in areas where you have previously felt inadequate. A teacher whose failing is a lack of gospel scholarship excuses his inability to inspire his MIA class by the fact that he can't compete with an intellectual element. What he needs to realize is that he has many strengths of his own and in capitalizing on these he need not compete with the strengths of others.

2. Understand that "there is no all at once." While it is only natural to feel that self-confidence comes from a recognition of one's strengths and limitations, and by making use of such strengths in the area of limitation.

3. Make a self-appraisal. Identify one characteristic in your personality which you feel needs improvement. Now ask yourself, "What can I do to improve this trait?" Now take one characteristic or trait you have of which you are very proud. How are you using it to help influence others?

4. Another interesting experiment with the same procedure is to ask yourself:

Don, a typical returned missionary, had everything it takes in the way of talent to achieve what he desired in life. Upon returning from his mission he outlined his goals to me one day. He first desired to obtain a college degree, then to specialize in dentistry, after which he hoped to start a practice in the town where he was raised. At the end of one semester, however, he had dropped out of school. "I decided that college wouldn't do me any good, it would take six to seven years out of my life at a time when I can be the most productive."

Who was Don trying to convince? Actually, this was his way of saying, "When the going got tough, I didn't have the faith and confidence in myself to meet the challenge so I gave up."

a. one reason why I am not as successful as I would like in my position,

b. one reason why I would make an excellent leader.

Now analyze each.

Which of the following best expresses the need for understanding self before becoming effective in leading others?

1. The persons who are most effective in working with others are cognizant of both their potential and limitations. (Turn to page 101.)

2. The people who are most effective in working with others are successful because they don't fear failure. (See bottom of page.)

Did you say, "The people who are most effective in working with others are successful because they don't fear failure"?

There are few effective leaders that don't have fears of failure. This is normal. Experience shows that the more successful leaders are willing to acknowledge their weaknesses and fears to those who work close to them. In this way they are able to use the strength of others to compensate for their weakness in the organization. It has been found that these men are the most spiritual in that they acknowledge to the Lord their weaknesses and ask him for his sustaining power to help them be successful. (Please see No. 2 above.)

While serving as an Institute Coordinator in Southern California, a new Institute Director was assigned to the region. He was a very talented young man, but was very concerned as to whether he would succeed. After he had been with us a short time, he came into the office one day and asked if he could be transferred back to his old assignment. "Brother Dunn," he said, "I feel like a failure—I haven't done anything to improve the program. How can I be sent back and save face?" What do you do with a worker when he gives you a request of this nature? Do you let him go and let him feel like he has failed, or do you work with him? I tried to give him every encouragement possible, but after our meeting he wasn't completely converted to the idea of staying. He said he would give it a second try but he wasn't sure he could do it.

About two weeks later, we held a faculty meeting with the Institute personnel. I remembered what this young man had told me, so I asked him to come up in front of the group. As he did so I suggested to the faculty I wanted to try something new and that we would periodically do this with each other. I then asked them to do two things: One, to identify a strong trait or asset in the man before them, something that they would like to emulate; and second, in identifying this trait, they were to tell how he could use the strength mentioned in working with others and how it could be utilized in building the program.

In turn I asked each of the directors and teachers to respond. As they did, the first said, "The thing I've noticed about you Brother________ is that you have one of the warmest handshakes I've ever experienced. If I had a handshake like yours, I would become personally acquainted with all the Latter-day Saint students I could. I would greet them warmly with that handshake and then I'd invite them into the program. If you'd take ten student names this week and try this experiment I

Did you say, "The persons who are most effective in working with others are cognizant of both their potential and limitations"?

You are right! These people have found that discouragement is the main barrier to achieving their potential goals. To offset this, they have made an honest appraisal of their strengths and limitations. Then they have used their strengths to help overcome limitations. This, they have found, gives them a better understanding and tolerance toward others weaknesses.

Now let's consider why people behave the way they do.

Why People Behave the Way They Do

Abraham Maslow, a renowned psychologist, tells us that the reason people behave the way they do is because of their wants and desires. It has been his experience that every persons' behavior is in response to his needs. (The meaning of the term "need" is something more than a deep craving or longing desire. A need is something that is essential to his physical, emotional and spiritual well-being.) He classifies these needs or wants from the lowest to the highest in the following order: The first is the person's physiological and safety needs. These, of course, are the most dominant and consist of a person's want for food, shelter, protection from danger, and threat. The next level of "wants" is the social and love needs. If a person's basic physiological and safety needs are satisfied, there will emerge the "love and affection and belongingness needs." These needs are acceptance and the giving and receiving of love. If a person is obstructed in the realization of these needs, maladjustment in the personality usually occurs. Next, he stresses the esteem needs, the desire for think you would have marvelous results." Everyone present agreed. In addition, a dozen or more suggestions of this type were offered.

When the session was over, this new director went back to his campus and tried what was suggested. He doubled his enrollment in two weeks and in time became one of our more successful men. The point is that he had capitalized on his strength. It didn't eliminate the fear, but reduced it to the proper size.

achievement, confidence, reputation and prestige. This is the person's desire for self-importance. If not satisfied, the person develops feelings of inferiority and helplessness. The highest need is the desire for self-fulfillment, that is, the desire to be what one is capable of becoming. This need is found in a person's longing to be creative, his craving for self-development, and his attempt to realize the best of his potential.

If an individual does not satisfy his wants or needs on a lower level, the higher needs can never be realized.

The challenge of leadership is to provide opportunity through programs and personal experiences which will help the individual realize his highest potential. To do so, we must be conscious of people's wants and desires, and we need to continually ask ourselves *why* they behave the way they do. What needs or wants is the individual attempting to satisfy? How can I help this person satisfy his needs so that he may realize the greatest potential in himself?

The late apostle, Adam S. Bennion, was noted for his sincere love for others. He was a master at making an individual feel important. How did he do it? He took a personal interest in every individual he met. To illustrate: When he went into any mission, he would greet the missionaries prior to their testimonial meeting in this way, "Brethren, I have in my hand a little black book. In here I have the recorded testimony of every missionary I've ever heard bear his testimony since I've been an apostle. I can do this because I write shorthand. What do I do with your testimony? If I'm ever in your home stake speaking at a conference, I'll tell them I've just been in your mission. Then I'll say, 'If you want to hear the testimony of Elder so and so, I have it in my little black book.' " Not only did his system pay off in terms of the sense of concern he conveyed to each individual missionary, but it had a great influencing factor on people in the home stake of that missionary.

On one occasion, he had just returned from the West German Mission and gave the invitation to all parents of missionaries in that mission to come up afterward and hear the testimony of their son or daughter. One couple came up and said they would like to hear the testimony of their son. He found out his name and looked in his little black book. "Are you certain you would like to hear his testimony?" he asked. "Why yes," said the mother, "is something wrong?" "It could be!" replied Brother Bennion. "Let me read his testimony. 'Brother Bennion, I'm looking forward to the day when my dad will show he loves mother and myself enough to take us to the temple to be sealed.' " With tears in his eyes, the father said, "He'll never have to worry about it again, Brother Bennion." Before he died, Brother Bennion had the privilege of sealing the family together in the Salt Lake Temple.

Too often we fail in a leadership capacity because we are not conscious of the needs of others. Or stated another way, we only succeed in a leadership capacity to the extent that we are conscious of the needs of others and satisfy those needs realistically.

The following is an example of a problem one church leader faced. What are the causes for this boy's behavior?

> Dee was a tall, strapping boy of 16. To look at him you would have thought him to be much older. When Brother Andrews was called to be the quorum advisor, Dee appeared to be the most quiet of all the boys. It soon became evident that he was the biggest trouble maker Brother Andrews had in class. Dee didn't say much, but how he could disrupt a class! On one occasion he took out a long handled knife and commenced to stick it in the floor. It was not infrequent that he would poke or jab the boy sitting next to him. To save the class, Brother Andrews thought it would almost be better if the boy wouldn't come to priesthood. He decided, however, that he would try to get close to the boy.
>
> He found that Dee came from a home where the mother and father fought continuously. The father would frequently take opportunity to belittle him or depreciate his worth. Dee, on several occasions, had run away from home. It was also found that Dee was the only boy in the class that came from a rural area. All the other boys lived in town.

Which of the following best describes why Dee behaves the way he does?

1. He is striving to meet some basic need or want that hasn't yet been satisfied. (Turn to page 107.)
2. He is an "immature" person who comes from poor environment. (Turn to page 107.)

THE NEEDS OF ALL OF US

1. We need food, protection, shelter and good health.
2. We need others to take notice of what we are and what we have accomplished.
3. We need to be accepted by others as an individual of worth.
4. We need to give and receive love.
5. We need to feel we are making a contribution of worth to others.
6. We need to develop the best that is in us by living principles of righteousness and having the influence of the Holy Ghost to guide us.

Did you say, "He is an 'immature' person who comes from a poor environment"?

Well, that's one way of looking at it. But let's consider this point of view. After you label a person "immature" or his environment as "poor" what have you said that explains the *reason* for his behavior? And what can you *do* to help him satisfy his wants if you don't know what it is that is causing his behavior to be what it is? This answer doesn't help you much toward this end does it? (Please return to page 105 and select the other alternative.)

Did you say, "He is striving to meet some basic need or want that hasn't yet been satisfied"?

You are absolutely right! Apparently you understand that people do what they do and say what they say because of an inner want or desire that remains to be satisfied. As a result of this point of view, this is what happened in this true story.

> Brother Andrews found, after visiting Dee on several occasions at his home, that he had a great love for horses. He also found the boy to be extremely talented in horsemanship. His behavior now made sense. The boy was fighting for recognition and acceptance among his peer group.
>
> Several weeks passed. Then at one of the quorum meetings it was suggested by the quorum secretary that they have an outing. The quorum secretary asked for suggestions and none of the boys showed much enthusiasm. "How would you fellows like to learn how to ride a horse, and perhaps go into the

When just a boy of 13, I came to know personally the great baseball player, Lou Gehrig of the New York Yankees. One day as I was "shagging" baseballs during a practice (giving the balls that are hit to the field back to the pitcher) Gehrig came to bat. Among Gehrig's great talents as a ball player, the thing that stands out most in my mind about the man was his sensitivity to the needs of others. Sensing my desire to be a ball player one day, and wanting to give me the encouragement, he motioned the pitcher off the mound and said, "Let the kid pitch to me." The pitcher on the mound, a "star" in his own right, and what ball players call an "old pro," said he didn't have time for kids on the field. "You heard me!" Gehrig called back, "let the kid pitch." The pitcher reluctantly handed me the ball and walked off the mound, and I stepped up to pitch to my boyhood hero. As I did so, Gehrig, who holds the record of playing the most consecutive ball games in the major leagues, sensed my nervousness. "Just relax Paul," he called to me. After hitting several pitches into the outfield, Gehrig swung hard at one and missed. "Nice shot Paul," he called back. "Give me another." It gave me confidence. After pitching to him, he called me to his side and said, "You've got unusual control for a boy of your age. While there is a lot you have yet to learn, if you'll continue to improve, you'll make it." Do I need to tell you how I felt? It was one of the greatest days of my life and one of the important factors that encouraged me into professional baseball. All because a great leader took time to be interested in a self-conscious "insignificant" boy of 13.

mountains?" suggested the advisor. The response was good. "Yeh, but where are we going to get all the horses?" asked one boy. Another inquired, "Who's going to teach us?" "I think that can be worked out," said the advisor. "Are you willing to go and support the activity?" The boys agreed. "Well," said the advisor, "Dee here is an expert horseman. I personally have never seen any better! Would you be willing to teach these 'drugstore cowboys' how to ride, Dee?" "Sure," he replied.

The activity proved a great success, but more important, Dee had the opportunity to show his ability and make a worthwhile contribution. Other activities followed where Dee was given recognition. The boys began to respect Dee and several came out to his farm with their cars to include him in their activities. Not only did Brother Andrews solve a serious discipline problem, but he saw Dee become a young man who faithfully represented the Church on a mission. In a different way the leader of these boys needed to know as much about every other boy as he did Dee.

How to Effectively Meet the Needs of Individuals

Working amiably together is important in church work because it is voluntary and idealistic. We need to practice looking for qualities in others as well as ourselves which develop good will. Here are a few suggestions:

1. Train yourself to be interested in people—to like them—to have a genuine respect for their ideas and feelings (even though you may not always agree).

A strong leader is often greatly admired, but he is also loved and followed if he knows how to involve other people and give them the feeling that it is their work, their organization, their cause. There is little interest in being a blind follower, or simply an obedient servant. People enjoy belonging to and working with the group. They love their own ideas.

Why do people need to be involved? There are sound reasons why creative participation by all officers (members also) is satisfying to them. It satisfies man's basic psychological and spiritual needs.

1. Man needs to belong to others. Above all else he needs to feel wanted, needed, loved and accepted by other human beings. This need is satisfied, not by sitting on a chair on row three or even row one, listening to others, but by feeling part of the group through self-expression and by receiving approval of others.

2. A second basic need in human nature is to be creative. Watch a child if you doubt this. Man is a child of God, the great Creator of the universe. Man was made not simply to be acted upon, but to act, to be productive—creative in his own right. As an officer or member of an organization he needs to feel his own fruitfulness, his own creativity, to grow and to rejoice in his own labors.

3. A third basic need is a feeling of one's own worth, self-esteem. This comes largely from achievement and from being loved, trusted, and respected by others. People need desperately to be successful, to have a "place in the sun."

4. A fourth basic need is response. People hate apathy and indifference; they would rather have a fight. They like their fellow men to respond to them in feeling and thought—to react to their hopes, fears, and aspirations.

2. Help your co-workers feel a sense of creative achievement by helping you, the leader, evolve the program.
3. Give people definite responsibilities and reasonable freedom to execute them.
4. Give credit where credit is due. Use "we" more than "I." Compliment people for work well done. Express appreciation.
5. Compliment people on their strong points. This is more effective than criticism though on occasion this is needed. People tend to measure up to other peoples' opinions and expectations of them.
6. Don't do anything you can get others to do; accept your share of the "load." Others like to contribute and achieve. Let them do it. Keep in the background as much as possible.
7. Respect individuality. There is more than one good way to do most things. Even if your way may be best, others learn most by doing, and even by making some mistakes.

Listed below are the three common reasons why some leaders fail:

1. The leader considers the program more important than the individual.
2. The leader considers group conformity to be more important than allowing for individual expression.
3. The leader manipulates others with whom he works in order to satisfy his needs instead of showing a sincere concern for others.

Let's consider what you, the leader, can do to prevent this happening.

"Men are more important than tools. If you don't believe so put a good tool in the hands of a poor workman."

People Versus Programs

All too often, leaders regard the program as being more "sacred" than the individual. They fail to remember that the program was created to meet the needs of the individual. The program should be followed, but the individual should be kept uppermost in mind. Let's illustrate: A certain organizational manual outlined the

Your object "People" are more important than programs.

program to be followed for a certain age group. The program outlined was excellent for most areas of the Church, but in the South Pacific, the suggested material did not fit the needs. When it was suggested that the organization adapt the program within the framework of the particular organization involved, the local leader responded, "Oh! do you mean we can do that?" NOTE CAREFULLY what was said, "Adapt the program *within the framework* of the organization involved." That does not mean we throw the program out, or change it, but that we gear it to the individuals and locality involved. Upon returning to the area some six months

"Remember, people are our most important product."

later, the leader reported that he had never seen such a change in the response of the people to a program. May it always be remembered by those in leadership positions that the development of the individual soul is the purpose of any program in the Church.

Individualization Versus Group Conformity

The one single factor which promotes effectiveness in working relationships, be it a home, a classroom, a church organization, or a business corporation is the individual's sense of worth in making a significant or unique contribution to that organization. When he is forced to "march in step" with every program, he inwardly, and not infrequently outwardly, rebels. The reason for this was stated many years ago by the French writer, Doudan. "Everything without tells the individual that he is nothing; everything within persuades him that he is everything." Emerson put it this way, "Every great man is unique." It recalls to mind the personal experience in the military service. Of necessity the military is concerned with building a "fighting machine" that functions as *one* unit. There is no room for uniqueness or expression of individuality. The sergeant's voice was a constant reminder that you, as an individual, were nothing. The "gripes," so associated with military discipline, were symptoms of what the individual was really trying to tell his superiors. "Look! Here I am, a unique individual. Why not treat me as one." While this may not be practical for a military organization, it is essential for the church organizations.

Here are some examples that may give some insight as to how to make others feel unique.

One stake president found people behave more co-

Be interested in others; interested in their pursuits, their welfare, their homes and families, their personal interests, habits, hobbies; the things they have done; the things they own, their knowledge, opinions, their names; the people and things they revere; their wants and needs. Take the trouble to exhibit your respect for their interests. Let every one you meet, however humble, feel that you regard him as a person of importance.

operatively when they feel their job is absolutely essential to the functioning of the whole organization. Before he tells the individual called about his specific duties, he takes the time to explain what the stake is attempting to accomplish and how his assignment fits into the total picture. He then tells the person *why* he is being called to the job and what unique talents he feels he has and how these attributes will enable him to accomplish the work. Then the leader explains the specifics of the assignment and the expectations he, the president has, for minimum performance of the job.

Sincere commendation for improvements is a tried and proven method of helping others to feel their uniqueness. All that is needed is a simple, sincere expression. "I want you to know how much we appreciate what you have done in your assignment. We want you to know that your contribution hasn't gone unnoticed or unmentioned."

One of the key ways to bring out the uniqueness in another is to capitalize on his strong points and minimize his weaknesses. This means you will need to observe and listen to what others have to say about him, in addition to making your own evaluation.

When it is found that an individual has a special talent or ability, give him an opportunity to use it or demonstrate it. This means that we look for abilities such as leading, directing, planning, presenting, drawing, painting, writing, handicraft, hobbies, etc., in addition to musical and speaking abilities.

Manipulation Versus Concern

I do not like thee, Doctor Fell
The reason why I cannot tell;
But this alone I know full well
I do not like thee, Doctor Fell
—*Tom Brown*

A new convert to the Church was called in by his bishop and asked to take a position in the priesthood. He was given special instructions that he should do all within his capacity to bring into activity several young men of priesthood age. One such young man was the son of one of the stake leaders.

When he went over to the home of this young man he found that the boy had no interest or desire in coming to Church. In spite of this boy's indifference, the priesthood leader persisted in coming back. He discovered that the boy's chief interest was rebuilding old cars. The leader learned a whole new vocabulary as the boy described the various parts of the automobiles. Pretty soon they were on speaking terms, then there was friendliness, and finally it got to the point where the young man would "kid" the priesthood leader about coming over in the attempt to get him active. The boy knew, however, that there was more to it than that.

One day when the leader came by for a visit he learned that his young friend wasn't home. The boy's mother asked the leader to wait for him in his room because she expected him momentarily. While he was waiting he noticed a Book of Mormon beside the boy's bed—one that had never been used to any extent. He was leafing through it when the boy arrived. After greetings were exchanged, the leader asked him if he had ever read the Book of Mormon, and the boy laughed and said, "No, I haven't done too much reading since dropping out of school." The leader rejoined, "I would like to give to you a personal challenge to start reading this book tonight. There are some people in here that I think would really fascinate you." The boy rejected the idea and with some disappointment the priesthood advisor left feeling that he had utterly failed in his mission. What he didn't know was that the young man accepted the challenge. Within three weeks he had finished the Book of Mormon. Shortly after he showed up at his priesthood meeting.

This couplet, penned many years ago, expresses the emotion that individuals sometimes "feel" when there is an attempt made to manipulate them. This manipulation may take the form of a feigned love or concern for the other, when in actuality the manipulator is only securing his needs. Or, it may be cloaked in the guise of learning another's ideas in order to make him feel he has had a "voice" in the matter when there is no intention of using his ideas. The person who manipulates others has found devices and techniques that he uses to serve the end of getting people to think well of him. Such devices may be the insincere smile, the compliment that says, "I enjoyed your talk," but meant, "I could hardly wait till you were through," or demonstrates enthusiasm and excitement over a project or program and then criticizes the innovator behind his back. What this person is trying to tell us, but can't is: "Look, I am really an emotionally insecure person—hungering for acceptance and recognition. This is my way of convincing myself and showing you."

Since the need to belong, to be accepted and recognized is such a prevalent want, the leader in the Church needs to be especially conscious of it in the people with whom he works. Some of the ways successful leaders have found to satisfy this need in others are suggested as follows:

First—discuss the desires and needs of your fellow workers. People will often reveal themselves in private talks when sincere interest in them is demonstrated. Four areas people are willing to discuss are: (a) their work, (b) their family, (c) their childhood, and (d) their hobbies or interests.

Second—people react favorably when they feel they have a vital role to play in the organization. Obtaining suggestions from workers on how the organization can be improved, is an excellent way to fulfill basic

Some time later during priests quorum activites the boy got up after several talks had been given and asked if he could express himself. Consent was given. He said with tears in his eyes, "I am sure that it is a shock to many of you that I have come tonight. There isn't much in my life that I have to be proud of—but just recently I was given the challenge to read the Book of Mormon, and I just want you to know, I know it is true, and I have come to a conviction within my heart that what I have been doing is wrong. I want you all to know that from this day forth you are going to notice a great change in me as a person." He then gave tribute to this priesthood leader who had taken the time to show personal concern. The boy later went on a mission and became most successful in his particular mission among the Lamanites. His whole life had been changed as a result of a leader showing concern for one boy. How many lives have been affected as a result of the leader's concern? Who can say? The young man in this story, however, has influenced a great many others into the Church of Jesus Christ.

needs and whenever possible these suggestions should be implemented. Then make certain that credit for the suggestions is given to the person who made them.

Third—develop the habit of thinking from the other person's point of view. It is a good idea to ask yourself, "How is this person reacting to this situation? What want is he trying to satisfy? What can I do to help?"

A bishop who successfully advanced all of the 52 Aaronic Priesthood members under his charge to the Melchizedek Priesthood credits his success to working from the boys' needs rather than the desires for high percentage activity. No one in the ward was able to reach one brilliant boy who felt there was no need for Church. The bishop, by applying the above, discovered the boy's real desires and needs and then moved ahead to fulfill them. Instead of trying to sell this boy on the value of church activity, the bishop instead called in a Latter-day Saint doctor to work with him. (The boy had a great desire to go into medicine.) Over a period of a year, the boy became active and is now a successful surgeon and active church member.

Thus it is seen that the underlying principle in working effectively with others in any leadership capacity is: *Discover the basic needs or wants of people, then provide them with some satisfaction in the areas of need.*

Let's suppose that a person who has served long and faithfully in your organization has become highly critical of the program and the way you are administering it. From the standpoint of helping this person, the best approach in your opinion would be:

1. Go to the leader over you and see if this person could be released. (Turn to page 123.)
2. Go to the person privately and say, "Your attitude is really affecting the program. I'd like to know what's wrong." (Turn to page 123.)

3. Go to the person privately and say, "You're a a person with a great deal of experience in this program and I understand that you have some real concerns as to what is being accomplished and how. How would you suggest it be handled?" (Turn to page 125.)

Did you say you would "go to the person privately and say, 'Your attitude is really affecting the program. I'd like to know what's wrong' "?

This is the direct approach all right! The idea is good but there are some limitations. (1) The person confronted has been indirectly told that the program is more important than he is, and (2) he is most apt to react with a defensive attitude such as, "What do you mean, 'what's wrong with me.'? It's the program and the leaders that are wrong!" His sense and worth have been threatened and such an approach only antagonizes him. (Please see No. 3 above.)

Did you say you would "go to the leader over you and see if this person could be released"?

That's one way to solve *YOUR* problem, but not his! His needs still remain to be satisfied. The symptom for this is his critical behavior. You might return and reconsider the suggestions given on pages 119 and 121 under the category, "Manipulation verses Concern," then read the problem again and select another alternative.

Did you say it would be best to go to the person and say, "You're a person with a great deal of experience in this program. How would you suggest it be handled"?

I'm glad you would—that is, providing it was done sincerely and with the intent to use his suggestions if applicable. What you did was compliment him on his background and experience. Further, you have indicated an interest to make use of his experience. The next step would be to implement his suggestions and then make certain he gets proper recognition for his ideas.

Let's try another example. Let's suppose that a person in one of your organizations comes to you and expresses how poorly he has done with his assignment. From the standpoint of his needs, what would be, in your opinion, the best thing to do:

1. Allow him to be released, expressing thanks for his efforts. (See below.)
2. Determine the reason for his sense of failure and make an attempt to capitalize on his strong points. (Turn to page 127.)

Did you say you would "allow him to be released, expressing thanks for his efforts"?

This is a good way to eliminate an ineffective person from your organization, but often defeats what you are trying to accomplish. He will leave with a sense of failure.

Usually, when a person comes to a leader and expresses failure, it's his way of asking for help and support. If released at that point, his sense of failure is confirmed. It is usually best to find his strong points and show him how these can be utilized in his assignment. (Please see No. 2 above.)

Did you say you would "determine the reason for his sense of failure and make an attempt to capitalize on his strong points"?

This is usually the best method because you are helping the person develop and at the same time provide for his higher needs. As an example, a Sunday School secretary came to her bishop expressing extreme discouragement with the way she was doing her job. She couldn't get others to cooperate with her. Most of her time was being spent in tracking down the attendance rolls for each class.

Her bishop gave her assurance that the assignment was difficult. Then he said, "The thing I have noticed about you is your meticulous concern for accuracy in what you do. I don't believe I've ever seen such concern for church records. I think that much of your frustration stems from not being able to collect all the attendance rolls, thus giving an incomplete picture of the ward attendance. Am I right?" She agreed that this was the problem. After some discussion on the problem, the bishop suggested that she arrange to have all class secretaries pick up the attendance roll from her at the preparation meeting. Then, they were to bring her that roll directly following the class at a designated place. This would eliminate her disrupting the class lessons and would permit her to obtain every one of the rolls each Sunday. As she implemented this suggestion, she found a great deal of satisfaction in her assignment.

CHAPTER 3 SELF-TEST

Here is a short self-test to help you summarize and apply the significant points of this chapter. If you need help, refer to the designated pages.

1. There were four suggestions made to help you overcome the fear of failure. What were they? What can you do that you are not doing now that can help you to overcome fear? (Page 97.)
2. People's behavior is sometimes difficult to understand. What did you learn that will help you to explain the reason why people behave the way they do? (Page 101.)
3. What are some of the most important needs to all people? What can you do now that you haven't been doing to help others in your organization fulfill their needs? (Page 109.)

Chapter 4

THE MAN WHO KNOWS HOW TO CALL OTHERS TO LEADERSHIP OPPORTUNITY

At the completion of this chapter, you should be able to:

1. Explain how you would select another person for an important church assignment.
2. Describe the ideal conditions that make a call to a church position more impressive.
3. Explain how to issue an effective call to responsibility in terms of the following:
   - a. creating the atmosphere for the call and interview,
   - b. making the call important to the person,
   - c. conducting an effective interview.

Chapter 4

THE MAN WHO KNOWS HOW TO CALL OTHERS TO LEADERSHIP OPPORTUNITY

How to Select the Right Person for the Job

The Challenge

Every year in the priesthood and auxiliary organizations of the Church thousands of wonderful, talented Latter-day Saints are called to leadership positions. It is not uncommon to hear those who are called express feelings of anxiety and concern with statements like: "I surely can't see myself in this position. I wonder where he got his inspiration for this call," or "I can't teach, they must really be scraping the bottom of the barrel to have asked me. In other words, too many people who are asked to staff our organizations feel that their calling has been one of expediency, rather than a prayerful, ponderous selection under the inspiration of the Lord. We can take the most capable people and place them in jobs simply to fill vacancies, but if proper thought hasn't been given to job requirements and matching abilities to assignments, with spiritual confirmation received from the Lord, we then contribute to their frustrations and fear of failure.

"Do not disparage others, but help and encourage them instead."

"Be kind. Nothing is so beautiful, no quality so irresistible."

"Courtesy is a great lubricant."

"Who me"! I'm not qualified.

Proven Methods of Selection

Many church leaders have found the following steps essential to the selection of the *right* person for the job.

1. Determine first the requirements of the job and the desirable qualifications a person should have to fill the assignment. For example, let's assume we are attempting to fill the position of a ward speech director. Those responsibile for such selection, in this case the MIA presidency, would meet together and give consideration to the following desirable requirements for the position.

a. A speech director should have a fair ability to communicate with others.
b. He should display poise and confidence in speaking ability.

c. Training would be helpful, though not essential.
d. The person above all, should have a desire to help others improve their speaking ability.

2. With job description in mind, the next step is to give prayerful consideration to *every* person eligible for such a position. This step will eliminate all those who are talented in other areas, but not suited particularly for this assignment.

3. After determining that there are several candidates that might qualify for the position some leaders have found it very helpful, at this point, to conduct a preliminary interview with the individuals. This is especially helpful when the persons being considered are not known to the officers. One of the usual procedures is to invite the person in, and ask whom he might recommend to fill the assignment. When certain names are suggested, the individual might then be asked why he or she would recommend these individuals. Discerning leaders are sensitive to the candidate's attitude toward the assignment. Some leaders might ask the candidate, "How would you feel about being called to this position?" The response of the person usually reveals his willingness to accept or reject a call. At this point, it is important to mention to the individual that a decision has not been made as yet, and the presidency or leader doing the selection will want to give the matter further prayerful consideration. It might be said this way: "We certainly appreciate your willing desire to serve your Father in heaven, Sister Brown. As we mentioned to you, a decision has not been reached as to the person to be called. The decision will be made after we go before the Lord in prayer. We appreciate so much your recommendations and fine attitude. Thank you for coming to see us."

4. The final step in the choice of a person being considered is to obtain the inspiration and confirmation

Shortly after being sustained as one of the General Authorities, I was assigned with a member of the Twelve to assist in the creation of a stake. In so doing, the thought occurred to me, "What a choice privilege this will be! I'll be able to sit back as a student and watch how an experienced leader handles such an important assignment and conference." What I didn't know was that he had the same thing on his mind. It was a spiritual experience of a lifetime.

Shortly after our arrival we began the task of selecting a president. After many hours of personal interviews the presiding authority asked that I give prayerful consideration to the brethren who had sat before us and, after consulting the Lord, to list three names in order of my preference as to who ought to be the stake president. He counseled me to let the Spirit of the Lord direct. "I'll do the same," he said.

Soon after retiring to a secluded room, I knelt before the Lord and asked for his Spirit and guidance. I knew that we were only servants on his errand, and that if a choice were to be made, it would be through inspiration. After listing the three names in order of my deep impression, I then took the list to the Apostle. He was waiting for me, and when I entered he inquired, "How do you feel about the names?" I replied that there was a feeling of assurance. He then said, "Place your list on the desk face down." He did the same with his. "Now let's ask the Lord for final confirmation." We knelt together and he gave one of the most humble prayers I had ever heard. We arose, and he said, "Do you still feel as assured?" "My feeling hasn't changed," I replied. "Let's compare the lists then," he said. We turned the lists over and compared them. *They were identical.* Even more miraculous was the order of preference, which was exactly the same.

of the Lord. After the candidates have been considered or interviewed by the presidency, bishopric or superintendency, the leaders should pray together that they might be guided in their selection. When a selection has been made, again the name of the person should be brought before the Lord for confirmation. If the leaders still feel impressed that this is the person the Lord wants for the position, the *right* one has been selected for the responsibility.

Some time ago, a man was called to be a Sunday School superintendent in his ward. Following his call and acceptance, his bishop told him that the bishopric had two fine men in mind for his assistants. The bishop offered to interview each of the men for the superintendent.

Which of the following, in your opinion, would best illustrate the approach that would determine the proper selection of this man's assistants?

1. The superintendent should thank the bishop for his help, but request that he would like to give the matter his prayerful consideration first. (See below.)

2. He should thank the bishop and have the men promptly interviewed so that the positions will be filled. (Turn to page 141.)

Did you say, "The superintendent should thank the bishop for his help but request that he would like to give the matter his prayerful consideration first"?

This is exactly what this brother did!

(Turn to page 141 and continue.)

A choice friend and neighbor's experience in receiving a call is an all too common experience in the Church. Just after a long fast and testimonial meeting, he was nabbed by a member of the stake presidency and asked to step into the bishop's office. They accorded him all the courtesy and respect of a brother in the gospel about to be honored with a new assignment. They asked him to be seated, and then in a very dignified manner called him to be an elder's quorum president. My friend was thrilled to accept the call. Then, as an effective stake presidency should, these brethren carefully interviewed him and then explained the nature of the assignment to him. An hour later, after being thoroughly interviewed and committed to his new responsibility, Tom left the office. Only one thing had not been taken into consideration—a very important thing. You guessed it, it was Tom's family out in the car!

Have you ever waited in a car for one hour on a hot Sunday afternoon with five hungry children crawling over the front and back seats, asking every two minutes, "When's Daddy going to come so we can go home?" Do I need to tell you how his wife, Linda, felt when he finally appeared on the scene? If there was ever any pride or excitement that Tom wanted to share with his family, it was the thrill he had just received regarding his new call. His wife, who is as dedicated and committed to the Church as any woman I know, couldn't have cared less about her husband's new assignment after what she had been through. Tom told me afterward that it took three months before his wife could share his feeling for the call.

Did you say, "He should thank the bishop and have the men promptly interviewed so that the positions will be filled"?

It's commendable to have that confidence in your ward leadership, but in this case, you just effected your own release. The bishopric has conferred upon you all the rights, privileges and responsibility connected with your position. You, therefore, because of divine appointment, are the person who has the privilege of selecting your assistants through inspiration from the Lord.

(Please return to page 139 and select the other alternative.)

Ideal Conditions for the Interview and Call

Where to Call a Person

Upon selecting an individual for a church position, it is only appropriate, courteous, and fitting to the dignity of the spiritual office and the person being called, that a private interview take place. This should be done in a private office, home or classroom where you may interview the person for worthiness, issue the call, and discuss the assignment without fear of interruption. Contrast this setting with the tap on the shoulder while you stand by the drinking fountain, the brief huddle in which you're requested to serve, and the reassuring pat on the back when you appear a bit bewildered with the newly acquired assignment. Is it any wonder why some hesitate to accept church positions with a sense of pride, security and enthusiasm.

"Glad I caught ya"!

When to Call a Person

Another important factor is the timing of the call. Wherever possible, and there are few exceptions to this, the call should be issued to the person at a time when his partner and members of the family might be present. Here are some suggestions in arranging such an interview.

1. The individual should first be contacted in person or by phone and asked to arrange a time when he could come to the church office with his wife and older children. If the wife is being called, her husband should also be included with the older children. A time should then be arranged with the understanding that the interview will take from a half hour to forty-five minutes.

2. At the appointed time, the person being called should be invited into the office alone. The call would then be issued, the person interviewed, and a brief summary of his job description explained to him. Then

the wife and older children could be invited into the office and included in the commitment. (In the case of a woman it is wise to have two or more leaders present in order to avoid situations which could prove embarrassing or lead to gossip.) Such an interview might take place as follows:

Let's assume that a priesthood bearer in his early forties is being called as a counselor in a bishopric. He has been asked to bring his wife and thirteen-year-old son with him to see the stake president.

Stake President: Sister Moore and Mike, after a great deal of prayerful thought and consideration, your husband and dad has just received a wonderful calling. He has been called to serve as first counselor to Bishop Merkeley in the newly formed bishopric of the Hillsdale Ward. How does this make you feel? Aren't you proud?

Sister Moore: I hardly know what to say. I'm so happy for him. We always knew that Jim would some day be called to an important position. We know he'll do a fine job.

Stake President: I'm glad to hear you say that Sister Moore, because a great deal of his success in this assignment will depend on your attitude and willingness to support him.

Sister Moore: We know that president. We'll be only too happy to do all we can to assist him in this assignment.

Stake President: We appreciate that, Sister Moore. Now Mike, how do you feel about

	your dad being called into the bishopric?
Mike:	It's OK I guess. I think it will be fine.
Stake President:	Do you feel you can really support him?
Mike:	Sure!
Stake President:	Now Mike, I want you to know there will be many occasions when you will need to show by your action as well as your word that you really do support your father. What would you say to some of your friends who wanted you to skip a meeting that you knew you ought to attend?
Mike:	Well, I suppose I'd have to say I couldn't. While I know it will be hard at times, I believe I can do my part to show my willingness to support dad.
Stake President:	That's fine Mike. We appreciate that spirit. With such support, your dad can't help but be successful.

Privacy, proper timing, and family inclusion are the important conditions in creating a dignified climate for the interview and issuing of a call.

The ward Relief Society president has requested a certain sister to serve as Social Relations teacher. If you were the presiding officer, which do you think would be the most ideal condition to make her calling a memorable experience?

1. Call her on the phone and set a time when she and her husband could come in together for an interview.

2. Have her come into the office alone after a church meeting for a private interview.
3. Check and receive approval and support of the husband first and then call them in for an interview.

Did you say the bishop should "call her on the phone and set a time that she and her husband could come in together for a private interview"?

This is the most ideal situation: After issuing the call to the woman privately the husband could then be brought in and he included in the acceptance and commitment. Under the circumstances, he is more apt to give his support and assistance to the wife. (There may be occasions when the interview and call might be accomplished with both parties present. Turn to page 151.)

Did you say the bishop should "have her come in the office alone after a church meeting for a private interview"?

The private interview is certainly desirable, but one of the primary supporting factors of her success in her job has not been included. You're right!—her husband. Often her accomplishments are in direct proportion to the support given by her husband.

(Please review the above and select another alternative.)

Did you say, "check and receive approval of the husband first and then call them in for an interview"?

Right! numbers 1 and 3 are both correct. The approach used would depend on the individuals involved and local circumstances.

As I went to President McKay's hotel suite, he was sitting at his desk, diligently at work. He looked up and, noticing that I had arrived, stood and extended the most cordial greeting I have ever experienced. He said, as he looked into my eyes, "Brother Dunn, thanks so much for coming to Salt Lake."

Imagine that! Talk about graciousness and respect! He was thanking *me* for coming to see *him*.

Because of the weather I was wearing a topcoat. Before I sat down he insisted on helping me off with my coat. He then had me pull a chair alongside the desk. Instead of putting me out in front in a typical counselee-counselor relationship, he asked me to sit beside him. He turned his chair sideways so that we had face-to-face contact, and then he leaned back, just looking right through me as only he can do. With that wonderful smile on his face, he said, "Brother Dunn, tell me a little bit about yourself."

I couldn't even remember my name. I remembered vaguely I had a mother, so I started there and finally put my genealogy together. I could see he enjoyed my plight, because he sat there smiling very kindly.

After about ten minutes of visiting—just getting acquainted—I found myself more at ease with each passing moment.

Finally he said, "I guess you are wondering why I have asked you to come to see me."

The thought *had* gone through my mind. I said, "Yes, sir."

He said, "Brother Dunn, last December, as you know, we lost a great Latter-day Saint in the passing of President Levi Edgar Young. I am calling you this morning to fill the vacancy created by his death."

How to Interview and Issue a Call

Setting the Atmosphere for a Successful Interview

Basic to successful interviewing for church assignments is placing the person being interviewed at ease. You might accomplish this by talking briefly with him about his family, job or other interests. It's most essential, even though you are busy, to create an atmosphere of warmth and friendliness where the person feels free to discuss any problem. He needs to feel that your time is completely at his disposal. One leader recently indicated that he desired to speak with his bishop concerning a problem he had faced for years, but which he had hesitated to bring to the bishop's attention. When asked why he hadn't discussed his problem before, he responded, "The bishop always seemed too busy or in too much of a hurry!"

The typical church leader is under a great deal of pressure to accomplish his assignment. Because of this he needs to remind himself constantly that PEOPLE, not reports, buildings, or programs, are his primary responsibility and concern. Since many members of the Church don't often have the opportunity to privately talk with their presidents, bishops, superintendents etc., this "routine" interview from the leader's standpoint, may be a choice and thrilling experience to the member.

Many bishops and stake leaders recognize this and make an effort to give the individual their complete attention. Some have arranged to have a small table behind their desk on which they can temporarily place correspondence, reports, and other matters that otherwise might distract them from the interview. This also

When he said that, I had a feeling and an impression come over me like I have never experienced in my life. Spiritually I was out of breath. Having played professional baseball for a number of years, I have been hit in the midsection my share of the time. You brethren who have been so involved—maybe some of you good sisters—know how difficult it is to get your breath. This is exactly what I was going through—just gasping for air.

Then I made a comment that slipped out before I thought about it. I said, "President McKay, in all my life I have never once doubted your judgment or inspiration—until right now."

Even then he did not lose his sense of humor, but he grew serious. He raised his finger and said, "Now, Brother Dunn, the Lord has called you to this position."

For the next several minutes he interrogated me and my soul was laid bare. I got a glimpse into the eternities.

has the added benefit of creating an atmosphere of order and dignity. There is no substitute for personal attention.

How to Make the Call Important to The Person

Once a leader has received the assurance from the Lord concerning the call of an individual, it is essential that individual be told that his appointment has come from a divine source. The actual call may be given as follows:

> Brother Swenson, my counselors and I have met to give our most prayerful consideration to the man whom the Lord wants to serve as deacons quorum advisor. We have given consideration to many worthy priesthood bearers in the ward. We are impressed to call you to the position. Before doing so, we asked the Lord for guidance and inspiration and he has confirmed our choice. You are the man he desires to call to the position.

Before the individual is asked to commit himself to the assignment, he should be given a clear understanding of what is expected of him. He needs to know what the assignment entails, its importance in the overall program, and the specific duties. He also needs to understand the time, energy, and interest he must invest and the meetings he is expected to attend. Many potential problems may be solved during the interview and the issuing of a call. If a clear understanding is given and the individual commits himself to a particular standard of performance, his leader need only recommit him to this standard if he falls below what has been agreed upon. If a person is not willing to commit himself to a minimum standard of performance, the job cannot be done adequately. A minimum performance may include the following:

What a sacred privilege it was to meet with President McKay in the temple and to have him lay his hands upon my head and ordain and set me apart. Prior to the performing of the ordinance the President sat and counseled with me concerning the duties and responsibilities of my assignment. He shared many of his own experiences and taught many truths as they related to my call. As he concluded he committed me to the assignment by asking if I were willing to lay "all that I had on the altar of God." Then he asked me to express my own feelings—to bear my testimony.

I looked at him and told him how I felt in my heart—how I had struggled as a young person; how I had come to know that the Church had been restored and that there were living prophets; that God lived and that Jesus was the Christ; that Joseph Smith was called and ordained to restore the gospel again to the earth; and how I had come to know that he himself was a prophet.

For a moment he just sat and looked. Then he leaned back in his chair and broke the silence with this observation: "Brother Dunn, the Spirit has just manifested to me that what you have said is right. We will now proceed with the ordination."

He stood up, had me take his chair, and then he came around behind and invited others of the quorum to do likewise. Placing his hands upon my head, he ordained and set me apart for this particular calling. As he did so, he gave unto me a special blessing to bear witness to the divinity and reality of Jesus Christ as the Savior of the world. As he pronounced that blessing, the sure knowledge of what I am now saying came into my heart and soul to the point that I can testify to all who would hear that I know that God lives, that Jesus is the Christ, that there are prophets called and ordained to lead this people. I have had the privilege of being in the presence of such a prophet and of having the spirit touch my spirit, giving divine verification.

1. A willingness to be thoroughly prepared and to seek the help of the Lord in prayer.

2. A willingness to be in attendance at required meetings.

3. A willingness to set a proper example by living in accordance with gospel principles.

4. A willingness to invest the time and energy to "go the extra mile" when necessary in accomplishing the task.

5. A willingness to commit oneself to the assignment.

Let's follow Brother Swenson's call through the above steps by this sample dialogue.

"Before you tell us your feelings about accepting such a great responsibility, we want you to understand clearly what will be expected of you. As you may know, the boys' present advisor is moving out of the ward. He has been a dedicated man and has done a tremendous job with the deacons quorum. These boys are accustomed to the best, so it is going to require a great deal of work, study, prayer, and preparation on your part. Do you feel that you will be willing to do this?" (*First Commitment*)

"Well, bishop, I'll surely do my best."

"The assignment will demand your best and we're really depending on you. It will take a lot of your time. In fact, there will be times when you may feel other things are more important and there will always be the temptation to just get by. Besides teaching the lessons on Sunday morning, we want you to really get to know these young men—to be not only a teacher, but a friend, a counselor, and a part-time dad. You'll need to keep track of birthdays, piano recitals, Little League

ball games, Boy Scout advancements, and broken arms. Do you know that the Church could lose half of your class to inactivity before they reach the age of eighteen if you and others fail in your responsibility."

"Now we have an outlined list of all the meetings that will be held in the ward and in the stake which are designed to help you in this great calling. As you can see, there are a few."

"Whew! There surely are. Stake priesthood leadership meeting, ward priesthood leadership meetings. . . ."

"Well Jim, we want to impress upon you that *if* you accept this call, we are going to expect you to do it with quality and enthusiasm. Even more important, the Lord will be expecting you to do it. Now, we're asking you not to accept this assignment unless you really intend to do it right. How do you feel about this?" (*Second commitment*)

"I feel it's a great responsibility. I'll surely do my best."

"Will you attend *all* the meetings and do everything you can to touch the lives of these boys?" (*Final commitment*)

"Yes bishop, I will."

If a leader discerns hesitancy on the part of the person being called, he should determine whether this stems from a feeling of inadequacy which training will solve, or a negative attitude toward doing all that has been asked. If it is the latter, then it is generally unwise to try to "sell" him on taking the job against his will. Undedicated service is usually the by-product.

It was about 8:30 in the evening when the phone rang. I was pleased to hear the voice of our stake president on the line. "Brother________, I wonder if you and your wife could come over to the church office for a few minutes. We'd like to talk with you." When we arrived, a member of the stake presidency was waiting in the foyer for us. He welcomed us warmly, shook hands, and led us directly into the president's office. There we were greeted cheerfully again and shook hands with the other counselor and with the president. He then stepped to the door and left word with the stake clerk that we were not to be disturbed. Following a few minutes of visiting about family and other affairs, the president leaned forward looking me squarely in the eyes. "Brother________," he began, "we have been pleased with your work in the ward. Now we have another assignment for you. How would you feel about a change?" After committing ourselves to serve wherever needed, he spoke again. "Brother________, we are calling you to serve on the high council of this stake. Do you understand how important this assignment is?" Then he proceeded to explain in the greatest detail the magnificent responsibility and opportunity that would be ours in this new work. He was very careful to include my wife in each step, outlining her role as the wife of a high councilor. Finally he drew an impressive and inspirational parallel between General Authorities on a Church-wide basis and high councilmen in a stake, and stressed the importance of being called by the Lord to serve as a stake "General Authority." Then leaning back in his chair, he said, "Now Brother and Sister________, we would like to hear each of you bear your testimonies, if you will. You first, Sister________, and then your husband." When we had finished, the president turned to each of his counselors and had them bear their testimonies. Then he bore his own. Full of the spirit of the gospel

How to Interview Effectively

When an individual has committed himself to dedicated service in the assignment, the next step is to thoroughly interview him to determine his worthiness. All too often leaders *assume* that individuals are living the standards of the gospel so that questions are asked in such a way that the person doesn't bring out his problems or concerns. Here are several examples of this kind of questioning. "You are living according to the gospel, aren't you? Are you morally clean? I assume you're keeping the word of wisdom." This type of questioning technique *presumes* worthy behavior and frequently individuals, not wanting to disappoint their president or bishop, will answer the question according to the assumption. Better questioning technique might be illustrated as follows:

"Brother Swenson, we appreciate your accepting this position. Now as you know, it's important that any person being called to serve in such an assignment be throughly interviewed as to his worthiness."

"Yes, I know that bishop."

"Do you fully support and sustain the president of the Church, his counselors, and the other General Authorities?"

"Yes, I do."

"Do you fully sustain and support your stake presidency and bishopric?"

"Yes."

"Are you morally clean?"

"Yes."

"Do you know what I mean by being morally clean?"

themselves, they encouraged us to dedicate the rest of our lives to the Church and its work. What more needed to be said? We left the office hand in hand with overflowing hearts of gratitude to our Father in heaven.

"I think so."

"What do I mean?"

At this point the individual can reveal his true understanding as to the meaning of "morally clean" as he reacts to the question. This also gives the leader an opportunity to examine him further by asking added questions in areas that might need to be brought to light.

"Fine. Do you keep the word of wisdom?"

"Yes, I do."

"Do you know what is meant by keeping the word of wisdom?"

"I believe so."

"What do we mean?"

"It means abstaining from tea, coffee, tobacco and alcohol."

"Anything else?"

"I suppose using judgment and moderation in all things."

Here again additional questions can be raised as the individual shares his own knowledge and understanding.

"Is your tithing a full and honest tithe?"

"Yes it is."

"Are you honest in your dealings with others?"

"Yes, I try to be."

"Will you do your assigned responsibility with all diligence and effort?"

"I will."

I wish it were possible for every Latter-day Saint to sit in the presence of a prophet and have him search their heart, soul, and mind. Never before have I felt such a penetrating power. I got a small glimpse into the eternities as to what it must be like to give an accounting to the Savior. I know now, as I have never known before, the process by which we must account for those things which we have done or that which we have failed to do in this state of our existence. I think if every Latter-day Saint could undergo such an experience, it would change the attitude and action of all.

I do not have the ability to relate all that goes on in such an interview, except that it is a spiritual experience one can never forget.

"Do you keep the Sabbath day holy?"

"Yes, I do."

"Do you know what is meant by keeping the Sabbath day holy?"

"I think so."

"What do we mean?"

Again, as the person responds the leader has an opportunity to see just what his understanding of the principle is and whether or not additional questioning is necessary.

"It's been a privilege to call you to this assignment, Brother Swenson. We surely appreciate your fine example and willingness to do the Lord's work. Now, may we hear how you feel concerning the call and your testimony generally?"

At this point, the individual has the opportunity to bear witness to the truthfulness of the restored Church, the mission of the Savior, and the reality of a living prophet today. The family may at this point be appropriately included.

Which of the following illustrates the better procedure in issuing a call to the person selected for the assignment?

1. It is usually best to give the person a call to a job, and then gradually allow him to learn about his new assignment so he will not become discouraged and overwhelmed. (Turn to page 165.)
2. It is best to give the person a clear understanding of his assignment and obtain a commitment of his feelings and willingness to do the job before finalizing the call. (Turn to page 165.)

Did you say, "It is usually best to give the person a call to a job, and then *gradually* allow him to learn about his new assignment so he will not become discouraged and overwhelmed with it"?

The major weakness of this approach rests on the fact that you cannot hold a person responsible to accomplish desired goals if he has not been adequately informed of them. One can hardly be expected to measure up to the expectations of a calling without an adequate explanation of the responsibilities involved. This is one of the reasons why so many of our church workers become discouraged.

(Please return to page 163 and select the other alternative.)

Did you say, "It is best to give the person a clear understanding of his assignment and obtain a commitment of his willingness to do this before issuing a finalized call"?

Excellent! Apparently you have found that a leader can expect no more from a church worker than what the worker understands and is heartily committed to.

(Turn to page 167.)

How to Obtain a Sustaining Vote and Meaningfully Set Apart the Person Sustained

When the call has been finalized, two important steps still remain: first, the sustaining by common consent vote of the local church membership; and second, the setting apart by those in authority. It is important to see that the individual is given deserving recognition, and has an opportunity to further commit himself to serve. Some leaders ask the person being sustained to sit on the stand. Then as he is presented, he rises and can be seen by those who are to sustain him. Whether on the stand or in the congregation, it is good to have him stand that all may know exactly who is being sustained. It is necessary also to word the presentation in such a way that it is not the action nor the leaders that are being supported and sustained, but rather the person himself. For example, the officer might say, "It is proposed that we sustain Brother Jim Swenson to the position of the deacons' quorum advisor. All those who can sustain Brother Swenson in this calling, please manifest by the uplifted hand! All opposed by the same sign." Some leaders have taken this procedure one step further by requesting that the person briefly, but publicly, bear his testimony as his pledge of dedicated leadership.

Following the sustaining vote by the ward or stake, he is then set apart, or ordained as the case may be, by the laying on of hands. Although many suggestions might be given, what is of most importance is the individual himself. All blessings given should be personalized to the individual. Several church leaders, to emphasize the importance of the wife to the success of the man's calling, have requested that the wife and

children be present. Wives who have had this privilege express gratitude for being included in such a sacred moment in the lives of their husbands.

Following the selection, interview, and setting apart or ordination, the auxiliary executives or priesthood leaders should make an appointment to get together with the new worker so they can distribute manuals, supplies and other materials. In such a meeting opportunity is given to ask and answer questions, help with problems about the assignment and provide encouragement for further dedication.

CHAPTER 4 SELF-TEST

1. Describe the process of selecting a person for a church assignment. (Page 135.)
2. What are the ideal conditions that make the call to a church position meaningful and impressive? (Page 141.)
3. How does a person go about creating the proper atmosphere for the call? (Page 151.)
4. What are the important things to tell a person that will make his call significant to him? (Page 153.)
5. How should questions be worded in the interview to make them most effective? (Page 159.)
6. How does an officer ask the congregation to sustain a person who has been called? (Page 167.)
7. What are two suggestions that make the setting apart or ordination ceremony more memorable to the individual? (Pages 167-169.)

Chapter 5

WANTED
THE MAN WHO CAN PLAN, PREPARE AND PRESENT
MAKING THINGS RUN LIKE CLOCKWORK

At the completion of this chapter, you should be able to:

1. Write an agendum for a planned event or meeting.
2. Select the appropriate steps in preparing for an event or meeting.
3. Indicate what you can do to improve your presentations before others.

Chapter 5

THE MAN WHO CAN PLAN, PREPARE AND PRESENT

Preparation Precedes Power

Ever since I first heard the late Adam S. Bennion make an address, I've been an admirer. On one occasion I had the opportunity to ask him the secret of his artful presentations. Without hesitation he replied, "For every half hour on the platform, there are twenty hours you don't see of preparation." Among the great lessons learned from this man, this has been one of the most significant: "If you want to succeed at anything, take the time to do a job well."

If you're like most, you believe this axiom with all your heart. But, how does a person go about the planning and preparing process so that effective presentations are possible? The purpose of this chapter is to consider the basic ingredients of how to plan, prepare and present.

Why Plan

Knowing the "why" of anything we do is as important to the success of a task as the "how." It provides an individual, or an organization with a defined purpose for taking a particular course of action. For

Before beginning, PLAN CAREFULLY—

Planning takes no more energy than wishing—

IF AT FIRST you don't succeed, you're running about average—

Be glad about the other fellow's success. Study his methods—

Only failure can be accomplished without effort—

Great works are done by perseverance—

It wasn't raining when Noah started to build the Ark—

example, if you were to ask a baseball coach why he planned a particular strategy, he would tell you that it was to produce as many "runs" as possible. If you asked him why he wanted to do that, he would reply, "To win the ball game." Unless the "why" becomes defined in terms of a specific outcome desired, the course of action remains meaningless.

It is not only the responsibility of a leader to define for himself the "why" to a course of action he is planning to take, but to clearly define it for all those affected by the action.

How to Plan

1. *State Your Purpose in Terms of a Specific Goal*—It is helpful to a leader to state specifically the purpose of his action before setting down that plan. One of the best ways to do this is to state the purpose in terms of the desired action to be accomplished. This method is illustrated at the beginning of each of the chapters of this book. The essential characteristics of a well-stated goal are behavior desired, understanding and action wanted. Several examples of objectives applied to church programs might be:

> "At the completion of this presentation, the home teacher should be able to issue an effective challenge."

> "At the completion of this program, the participant should be able to speak more effectively before groups."

> "At the completion of this meeting, a person should be better able to define his assignment in relation to the Priesthood Correlation Program."

He who knows not, and knows not
    that he knows not, is a fool, shun him;
He who knows not, and knows that
    he knows not, is a child; teach him;
He who knows, and knows not that
    he knows, is asleep, wake him;
He who knows, and knows that he
    knows, is wise, follow him.

—Persian Proverb

2. *Evaluate Goals*—Goals should always be stated in terms of people. For example: One often hears that the purpose of home teaching is to teach the gospel. The gospel can be taught poorly or well, and in a way in which people will not like it, or will love it. Would it not be better to state the objective something like this: "The purpose of home teaching is to help families love and live the gospel of Jesus Christ more fully."

Goals should not be too general nor vague, but concrete and specific. For example: It is often said that the purpose of the Boy Scout Program is to build character in boys. This is acceptable as a broad, general purpose, but a scoutmaster, planning the year's work or his next scout meeting, must be far more definite and specific. He might well ask himself what qualities of character do my boys, ages twelve to thirteen, living in this ward or branch need most? He might with due thought, come up with two or three goals for the year such as: 1. To help each boy increase in his own self-respect and confidence; 2. To help each boy learn to say "no" to things which are momentarily attractive but not for his long-range good, and to say "yes" to things which are hard to do, but which will in the long run be for his good.

Church leaders and workers need three kinds of goals:

1. an over-all goal for all church work,
2. goals for this year, or for a specific period of time,
3. a specific goal for each activity, event, lesson or talk.

Lowell L. Bennion points out that the goals should:

1. meet the needs and interests of the people involved,

Creativity is stimulated by purposeful planning. Without the pursuit of goals, life is drab, quite meaningless, confusing, and might even be idiotic. When we have goals in view, our thoughts, feelings, and actions tend to organize themselves around these goals. This is true of church work as well as of one's private life.

There is no better first step in preparing a lesson or in planning an activity than to write down one's major aim in the class or function. The imagination is then stimulated to think of a great variety of means by which the goal may be attained. The creative person is very flexible in considering every possible means of reaching a desired goal. He can always check them for effectiveness and integrity before they are employed. He must have some flexibility in his immediate goals too, as long as they are consistent with fundamental goals indicated by the gospel.

—Lowell L. Bennion

2. be appropriate to the occasion and the organization which fosters them,

3. be clearly distinguished from method. (Six Fundamentals of Good Teaching and Leadership in MIA by Lowell L. Bennion.)

Think of goals in terms of people's needs. An example will help to illustrate: A young girl may not have the desire or see the purpose of attending MIA, but her support of the program will come as a result of having a need fulfilled through the organization. An effective teacher might express the goal of a lesson in terms of the girl's need in this way: "Janet, several of our girls would like to have a fashion show to demonstrate how to coordinate colors to the seasons. They also are interested in learning how to coordinate colors to one's complexion. Knowing of your interest and realizing how much you would contribute to the evening, we would surely love to have you with us. Would you like to come?" Even more effective is the invitation given to her by one of the girls her own age. In using this approach, however, the leader must make certain that the need to be fulfilled is real and that it relates to an area of interest.

An important thing to remember in the presentation of any goal is: A program imposed will oftentimes be a program opposed!

3. *Develop a systematic plan of presentation*—Whether an individual is teaching a lesson, conducting a meeting, or giving a talk, a systematic presentation of his ideas is essential to the success of that presentation. Earl Pullias says that the greatest mistake most of us make in presenting material is to present too much. We feel an obligation to cover all, and in so doing we are ineffective in what we treat. Instead we should attempt to present no more than two or three concepts.

One day a management consultant, Ivy Lee, called on Schwab, President of the Bethlehem Steel Company. Lee outlined briefly his firm's services, ending with the statement: "With our service, you'll know how to manage better."

The indignant Schwab said, "I'm not managing as well now as I know how. What we need around here is not more 'knowing' but more 'doing'; not knowledge but action. If you can give us something to pep us up to do the things we ALREADY KNOW we ought to do, I'll gladly listen to you and pay you anything you ask."

"Fine," said Lee. "I can give you something in twenty minutes that will step up your 'action' and 'doing' at least 50 percent."

"O.K.," said Schwab, "I have just about that much time before I must leave to catch a train. What's your idea?"

Lee pulled a blank 3 X 5 note sheet out of his pocket, handed it to Schwab and said: "Write on this sheet the six most important tasks you have to do tomorrow." That took about three minutes. "Now," said Lee, number them in the order of their importance." Five more minutes pass. "Now," said Lee, "put this sheet in your pocket and the first thing tomorrow morning look at item one and start working on it. Pull the sheet out of your pocket every 15 minutes and look at item one until it is finished. Then tackle item two in the same way, then item three. Do this until it is finished. Then tackle item four and so on. Do this until quitting time. Don't be concerned if you only finished two or three, or even if you only finish one item. You'll be working on the important ones. The others can wait. If you can't finish them all by this method, you couldn't with any other method either, and without some system you'd probably not even decide which are most important."

Elder Adam S. Bennion, phrased it this way, "Never develop more than three points from one idea." It may be your purpose in an organizational meeting to define the responsibility of an adviser to the Aaronic Priesthood adult by listing from one to three goals which would achieve maximum effectiveness. To illustrate—the presentation goal might be:

At the completion of this discussion, the advisor should be able to:

a. define his own role in the Aaronic Priesthood Program in reactivation,

b. write a plan for reactivating one man per month,

c. list the steps to be taken to ensure the realization of an active fellowshiping program.

Each of these three points would be elaborated upon through discussion, stories and charts. By using a written plan, you may re-evaluate your goal to determine whether you were successful and to what extent. In other words, was the adviser able to define his role in terms of reactivating adult Aaronic members? Was the adviser able to write down a plan for reactivating one man per month? Was he able to list the steps to be taken to ensure an active fellowshiping program?

If any one needs a written plan it is those who function in an executive capacity. One of the frequent complaints of those in executive positions is, "How can I do all that needs to be done?" Here is a simple system recommended by Ivy Lee, a management consultant:

a. Make a list of the six most important things you need to do tomorrow as a church leader.

b. Determine the relative importance of the six items and number them in order of importance.

"Spend the last five minutes of every working day making out a 'must' list for the next day's tasks. After you've convinced yourself the worth of this system, have your men try it. Try it out as long as you wish and then send me a check for what YOU think it's worth."

The whole interview lasted about twenty-five minutes. In two weeks Schwab sent Lee a check for $25,000—a thousand dollars a minute. He added a note saying the lesson was the most profitable from a money standpoint he had ever learned. Did it work? In five years it turned the unknown Bethlehem Steel Company into the biggest independent steel producer in the world; made Schwab a hundred million dollar fortune, and the best known steel man alive at that time.

c. Tackle, one at a time, each of the items in order of importance.

ARE YOU ALL THUMBS WHEN IT COMES TO KEEPING THINGS AT YOUR FINGERTIPS —

4. *Use an Agenda*—What has been said about the use of a written plan applies even more so to the conducting of an effective meeting. A meeting will fail in its purpose when the leader fails to define the objective and scope of the meeting to those involved. Cautions to observe in the planning of an agenda are these:

a. Be conscious of the time element. If the meeting is to last one hour, you will be able to handle effectively only two to four major business items. To attempt to crowd more items into that time will lead to the frustration of not being able to cover what was on the agenda, or give an adequate treatment to the listed items.

b. Send out the agenda to those involved in the meeting several days preceding the meeting. This allows them to give consideration to each item before they come to the meeting.

c. Those involved in a program should be given the opportunity of submitting items for the agenda. It should be understood by all those involved in a program that items will not be considered in the meeting unless they are a part of the agenda. Emergency items should always have a place.

d. The agenda should teach the purpose and function of the organization to the individuals involved in the meeting by the outlined presentation of business.

How to Prepare an Agenda

The word "agenda" means "things to be done." (Technically the singular has been "agendum," but through usage "agenda" is now also used in the singular.)

An agenda should not be just a miscellaneous listing of questions and topics any more than a meeting should be.

Which of the following would be the more effective agenda:

(MEETING) PRIESTHOOD EXECUTIVE MEETING

AGENDA Date________

I. Opening prayer

II. Minutes

III. Announcements

IV. Priesthood correlation program of ward:

A. The Priesthood Missionary Program

1. New contacts
2. Youth Missionary Committee events
3. Fellowshipping progress with new converts

B. The Priesthood Genealogy Program

1. MIA classes
2. 3rd and 4th generation program—report by high priest's group leader

C. The Priesthood Home Teaching Program

1. Report by assistant ward clerk for home teaching

2. Reports given by each priesthood leader

D. The Priesthood Welfare Program—(Relief Society president come). (Use outlined agenda in Priesthood Welfare Program.)

E. Issue of the day.

V. Closing prayer

Occasion Date

I. Greeting

II. Prayer

III. Minutes from previous meeting (Read and approved)

IV. Announcements (Things which require no discussion and can be disposed of quickly)

A.
B.
C.

V. Items of business (Things to be discussed and executed—usually quite a variety)

A.
B.
C.

VI. Issue of the day

VII. Closing prayer

Example 1

Date

WARD COUNCIL MEETING

I. Prayer

II. Minutes

III. Priesthood correlation instructions

A. Priesthood Welfare
B. Priesthood Genealogy
C. Priesthood Missionary
D. Priesthood Home Teaching

IV. Correlation of ward program

A. Auxiliary programs

1. MIA
2. Primary
3. Sunday School
4. Relief Society

B. Priesthood Activities:

1. high priests
2. seventies
3. elders
4. Aaronic Priesthood

a. adult
b. youth

C. Other organizational activities

1. Seminaries and Institutes
2. Music correlation in the ward

V. Special instructions and problems (Issue of the day)

VI. Closing prayer

Example 2

GOOD PLANNING PRODUCES SUCCESS

WHAT? (Goals)
WHY? (Justification)
HOW? (Methods)
WHO? (Personnel)
WHEN? (Timing)
WHERE? (Locale)

WRITTEN PLANS

LESS MISUNDERSTANDING
CLEARER PLANS
RECORD FOR REVIEW
PLANS ARE MADE
MORE CERTAIN SUCCESS
LEADERSHIP GROWTH
RECORD FOR FUTURE
LESS FORGETTING

Did you say the most effective agenda is "Example 1"? At least it is an improvement over no agenda at all, but even this outline lacks a proper format which will educate the members involved to the purpose of the meeting. (Please return to page 189 and see example 2.)

Did you say the most effective agenda is "Example 2"? EXCELLENT! Apparently you can see how this type of agenda can serve the purpose of educating the members of your group to the purpose of the meeting.

How to Prepare for an Event or Meeting

Preparation of Activities

Once a specific goal has been stated, and a written plan made for the successful realization of the goal, the next step is to make careful preparation for the presentation. This may involve, depending upon the activity, preparation in the following areas:

1. *Rehearsals*—This will be especially necessary when coordinated efforts of two or more individuals are needed to accomplish the task. The value of a rehearsal lies mainly in raising the actual performance to a minimum acceptable standard when the presentation is given. Most effective leaders carefully rehearse an individual presentation before it is given, to ensure an adequate performance in the presence of others.

CHECK SHEET FOR SOCIAL ACTIVITIES

Chairman____________________Date of Activity____________

Type of Activity________________________________

Location of Activity______________________________

ITEM	PERSON RESPONSIBLE	CHECK ON PROGRESS
I. Theme		
A. Decorations		
B. Entertainment		
C. Games		
D. Mixers		
E. Costume		
II. Location		
A. Reservation		
B. Lighting		
C. Public address		
D. Transportation		
E. Extra tables or chairs		
III. Music		
A. Band		
B. Records and equipment		
IV. Publicity		
A. Tickets		
B. Posters, flyers		
C. News articles		
D. Announcements		
E. Invitations		
V. Refreshments		
A. Food and drinks		
B. Cups and napkins		
C. Eating utensils		
D. People to serve		
VI. Photographer		
VII. Special guests and patrons		
VIII. Clean-up		

2. *Preparation of special visual aids or materials*—Frequently it is helpful to use graphs, charts, posters, or other audio-visual aids in making an effective presentation. It has been said that "quality isn't accidental; it is always the result of an intelligent effort." In making preparation, therefore, a leader needs to allow himself sufficient time to produce the highest quality of product of which he is capable.

If, however, a leader finds himself having a great deal of difficulty in producing such aids, it is an excellent opportunity to utilize the talents of others in the branch, ward or stake. Just because a leader may not have the personal talent to prepare the best quality aids which will assist him in his presentation, it is no excuse for not using them.

3. *Use of checklists*—It is almost mandatory to the success of an effective function that a leader utilize a checklist to ensure proper follow-through. A week-to-week checklist which sees a project or activity through to its completion ensures that important responsibilities are completed by certain dates. The checklist on the opposite page will illustrate various steps that one might follow to ensure the success of a church dance,

The Value of Pre-Planning

The preparation that precedes a meeting is extremely important and plans must be well laid and carefully detailed if the meeting is to be successful. It has been said, "the successful leader puts his head into a thing before he puts his foot into it." As leaders, before we put our foot into the door of the room where a meeting is to be conducted, we should have put our thinking into the things that are to be considered.

Imaginative Planning

Leaders should not be afraid to break with the traditions of the past if, in doing so, they have something better to offer. It is a very dangerous thing to find a good procedure, then do it that way continuously. Finding new and better ways of doing things not only develops leadership, but it makes leadership a more challenging and interesting experience. The leader in planning meetings should have the following question before him at all times: "What ruts have I gotten into?" Use imagination. Try something new.

Participation and Expression

We should utilize others in our meetings so that interest may be increased through participation and experience. Remember, we do not like to spend all of our time listening to others. We appreciate opportunities to express ourselves. The wise leader recognizes this and will utilize his associates in a variety of ways depending on the type of meetings. Good leadership demands the utilization and participation of all members of an organization from time to time in different numbers and in a variety of ways.

bazaar, or social. Successful activities just don't happen; they are planned that way!

4. *Proper spiritual preparation*—This is the most essential portion of the preparation phase. With the spirit of the Lord accompanying a presentation, individuals become motivated toward spiritual goals. Without this spirit, the presentation may be mechanically excellent, but yet lack the power which can carry a presentation into the hearts of the participants. Even the mechanical perfection of the famed Tabernacle Choir, is second to the success achieved in their spiritual preparation and presentation. What preparation does one need to make in order to obtain this spirit? The admonition of the Lord as applied to missionary work is equally applicable to every other phase of church work. "And the Spirit shall be given unto you by the *prayer of faith;* and if ye receive not the Spirit ye shall not teach." (D. & C. 42:14.)

Preparation for Meetings

Meetings, like activities, to be successful need specific goals. Once these goals have been defined, preparation to ensure the successful completion should be made in the following areas:

1. *Preparation for the members' physical comfort*—We so often take for granted the physical comforts of our buildings and it isn't until we experience an uncomfortable situation that we are brought to an awareness of how much one's physical surroundings and personal comfort can add to the meeting. Raise or lower the temperature 5° beyond what is normally experienced and the difference becomes immediately noticeable! An effective leader will make certain that such things as proper heating, lighting, and microphone equipment are in order before the meeting commences.

HOW TO PLAN A SUCCESSFUL ACTIVITY

4 weeks before event:	Plans for activity completed Member assignments made Invitations to special guests, stake presidents, bishops, school officials.
3 weeks before event:	Preparation of publicity material, posters, articles, flyers, mailers. Call photographer.
2 weeks before event:	Release of publicity material Sale of tickets begins Committees meet for review of assignments.
1 week before event:	Second release of publicity material Ticket sale continues with evaluation of effectiveness Member phone committees begin contacts Inactive members contacted personally Member committees meet for final review of assignments for social activity.
Event:	Organizational committees fulfill responsibility
Shortly after event:	Leader meets with organizational committees—activity is evaluated and members' contributions acknowledged. Letters of appreciation sent.

2. *Contacting the participants who will take part*—It is desirable to have any meeting planned as much as one month in advance so that the speakers and other participants can make proper preparation. At that time the specific goal of the meeting would be given to the participants. Some leaders have found it desirable to assign definite topics. (This would vary depending on the occasion.)

One week in advance of the meeting, the participants should be notified again so that they will be aware of their assignment. Conflicts and uncertainties can be eliminated at this point. Encouragement such as, "We're counting on you to do an effective job in motivating our youth," might be offered at this time.

3. *Publish a program*—To minimize the announcements over the pulpit, many wards and branches have found it most helpful to include these items in a ward bulletin to be distributed by the ushers. A deadline date for entries should be given to the various leaders of the ward organizations in order to avoid announcements being handed to the bishopric just prior to the meeting. There is nothing more distracting to a meeting than to have a leader try and read poorly constructed announcements on small bits of paper handed to him seconds before the meeting commences.

Publishing a printed program also gives the individual participant the deserved recognition for his part on the program.

4. *Setting a spiritual tone*—One of the most distracting things to a meeting is the officers making last minute preparation on the stand. It often gives the appearance of a football backfield in motion. Attention to all details such as passing of the sacrament, the invocation, benediction, and musical numbers should be taken care of well in advance of the meeting. The presiding officers should be seated on the stand at least

PLANNING A SACRAMENT MEETING

Purposes	*Methods*
1. To help people worship God.	1. Have chapel clean, attractive, well heated and ventilated. 2. No talking on stand. 3. Reverent, dignified administration. 4. No announcements unless they contribute to spirituality.
2. To help people renew and deepen their faith in Christ.	1. Educate Aaronic Priesthood boys in meaning and privilage of the sacrament. 2. Careful choice of music. 3. Timely remarks on occasion by bishop. 4. Build more of program around the Savior in speech and song.
3. To help people gain spiritual strength and motivation, such as (1) strength to resist temptation (2) courage to carry on, (3) peace of mind.	1. Inform speakers of this purpose. 2. Choose music well. 3. Develop a spiritual fellowship in the ward. 4. Let people give of themselves to the meeting.

—Adapted from *Leadership Training*
by Lowell L. Bennion

five minutes prior to the hour set for the meeting to begin. The reverence to be achieved in any meeting is in direct proportion to the attitude and example of the leaders.

Many presiding officers have found that the spiritual tone of a meeting is greatly enhanced when all participants meet together briefly for a prayer and last minute attention to details.

One other matter that can assist in setting a spiritual tone of a meeting is the function of the clerk. It is not uncommon for a speaker to be in the midst of a talk when the clerk steps out of his chair and goes into the audience to count heads. All eyes shift at once to the clerk. Whatever interest or attention has been created by the speaker up to this point is suddenly lost. In recognizing the importance of a clerk's task, a simple suggestion is here made to eliminate one of the most distracting features in any meeting:

In a sacrament meeting, for example, the clerk should know, by previous count, how many individuals could be seated in one row of seats (pews). He could then count the total number of seats (pews) to determine a full capacity audience. During the meeting he could then count the number of spaces not filled and subtract this number from the total capacity or add as the case might be, to ascertain the count of the membership present.

If it is a stake or district conference, the clerk could count the total number of seats available before the meeting, and then deduct or add accordingly to determine the exact number present.

By using this technique, the clerk can accomplish his task without leaving his seat, thus adding to the spirit of the meeting.

The following questions, and others, should be considered by the leader when planning a meeting:

What is the purpose of the meeting?

Is the purpose stated in terms of people?

Who will be present?

Is the meeting appropriate to the occasion?

Where will the function be held?

1. Which of the following best illustrates the steps in making preparation for a planned meeting?
   a. Publish a program, use a checklist, make preparation for members' personal comfort.
   b. Make preparation for personal comfort, set a spiritual tone, prepare visual aids.
   c. Preparation for physical comfort, contact participants, publish programs, and set spiritual tone.
   d. Publish a program, prepare aids, and set spiritual tone.
2. Which of the following best illustrates the steps in making preparation for a planned event?
   a. Rehearsals, preparation of aids to be used, and spiritual preparation.
   b. Checklists, rehearsals, prepare aids, and spiritual preparation.
   c. Rehearsals, published program, checklists, contacting those on the program.
   d. Published program, rehearsals and contacting those on program.

The best answer to question 1 is "c."
The best answer to question 2 is "b."

How to Improve Presentations

Getting Others Involved

The key to getting others "with you" is to get them

How to be Confused:	*How to Think Clearly:*
—Incomplete information	—Do I have all the necessary facts?
—Inaccurate information	—Are the facts correct?
—Failure to see others' point of view	—How does he see (or think about) these facts?
—Failure to sift facts from "hunches" or "opinions"	—Have I sifted the facts away from opinions?
—Failure to relate facts together in terms of their importance	—Which are the most important facts?

involved in the presentation. This can be done several ways.

1. Present a true life situation that relates to the group and have several members assume the roles of the individuals in the problem situation. For example: The Roberts Family has two teen-age youth who are not attending church. Have the home teachers demonstrate how they might be effective in motivating these young people.

2. Draw upon the resources of those most knowledgeable. Assume for example that you were making a presentation relative to the role of the priesthood in the Genealogical Program of the Church. The high priests group leader might be called upon to define his role in this program.

3. Allow others to bear testimony to the efficacy of the program. If the area of presentation is your specialty, it might be well to allow others to "toot your horn." Ofttimes a product of the program can be far more effective than the leader himself. An Institute graduate will often have a greater influence in "selling" the program to others because of his unbiased endorsement. People expect the leader to be enthusiastic.

4. Divide into work groups. This method of involvement is most useful when there are a combination of problems that demand solution, or when the total group is not affected by all the problems. In order that this be skillfully handled, discussion leaders need to be briefed on the problem, the time limits, and the reporting system. A stake priesthood leadership meeting is a situation where this method might be used. It is conceivable that the stake presidency might be concerned about priesthood activity in these areas: (1) the problem of inactivity among the teachers and deacons, (2) too few priests being eligible for mission calls, (3) bish-

Many things can be accomplished when people work together in unity of spirit and mutual loyalty toward a common goal. Leadership can prove that it is good leadership when it strives constantly to become better leadership. Good leaders can become better leaders by developing new leaders—and a leader, in my opinion, is one who never has to look behind him to know that he is being followed.

—Joics Stone

"An error doesn't become a mistake until you refuse to correct it."

ops not using the general secretaries to their best advantage, (4) no adequate adult Aaronic programs, and (5) the problem of the quality of instruction in the Melchizedek Priesthood quorums.

The stake presidency would introduce the problem to the total priesthood leadership assembled. Instructions might then be given for all advisers and bishop's counselors concerned with the problem of inactivity of deacons and teachers to meet with high councilman A; priests' advisers to meet with high councilman B; bishops and general secretaries and assistants to meet with high councilman C; adult general secretaries and assistants to meet with high councilman D; and all Melchizedek Priesthood quorum leaders and presidencies to meet with the stake president and high councilman E. It is understood that each of the high councilmen assigned to their groups would have had special training experience in working with their respective problem. Assignments will have been given several weeks in advance to those who are to participate in the various groups. Further instruction would include the time to be spent in the group, and how this discussion will be used to implement an improved program in each ward. As an example, the stake president might say, "Brethren, we want you to discuss the problem in your group and come up with several concrete suggestions on how to solve the problem. You will have 45 minutes in your assigned group. After you have done this, we desire each bishop to meet together with the total priesthood organization of his ward for an additional 30 minutes at which time the programs will be discussed and correlated. We would like a written report submitted to the stake presidency on the plans of each ward to solve the problems we have considered at this time."

Attitude

The conducting officer can be warm, friendly and yet purposeful and dignified. He should bring to his task a humble, reverent, prayerful attitude, and be guided by purpose and inspiration more than by rigid rules. (Read Moroni 6:9.)

Make Few Interruptions

Since the conducting officer is but instrumental to the purpose of a meeting, he should not interrupt the proceedings more than necessary. In regular meetings, such as Sunday School and Sacrament meeting, once or twice is all that he needs to speak. It is also appropriate if people can sing, pray, sing again and partake of the Sacrament without interruptions such as announcements and introductions.

Make Words Count

Words should really say something constructive. Some words that detract from the proper spirit of the meeting are:

> Rehashing a talk already given,
>
> Excessive praise or thanks to speakers and program members in sacred meetings. The purpose of the meeting is to honor God or Christ, not the speaker. Moreover, if he gives a good talk no praise is needed. If he gives a poor talk it will only prove embarrassing. We should not thank people for praying, nor should the Aaronic Priesthood be praised each time they pass the Sacrament. *This is their privilege.*

Making Presentations Meaningful

If you are called upon to make a presentation before a group, and there are certain things you want the group to remember, here are several suggestions that will be helpful:

1. *Use visual aids*—Facts and figures illustrated by charts, graphs, and art work will be retained longer and make a more significant impression than simple telling.

2. *Use a printed handout*—A mimeographed handout may be given to each member of the group following the presentation. This may be a written summary of what was said—just the salient points.

3. *Illustrate each major point or idea*—Until an idea can be taken from the abstract and translated into human experience, understood by all, the presentation will be ineffectual. The best resources one has are the personal experiences of those around him and his own personal life. In using examples, however, it is best to use "positive" illustrations that tend to encourage, build, and inspire rather than the "negative" which depresses. In other words, tell them how to improve through an effective illustration rather than giving a poor example of "how *not* to do it." Be cautious not to make the illustration bigger than the principle.

How to Conduct a Meeting

If you are called upon to conduct a meeting for the first time and you feel apprehensive and insecure, you have just joined the ranks of thousands who have felt the same. Of all the responsibilities in the Church, this is one of the most frightening, but at the same time vital, because by setting the proper atmosphere for a meeting, an individual's ability to commune with God

"Man is an imitative creature, and whoever is foremost leads the herd."

—Schiller

is enhanced. For this reason, the following suggestions are given to assist you in discharging this responsibility with a minimum of fright, but with maximum effectiveness.

1. *Pre-arrange all business, physical facilities, and the program*—Nothing adds more to the anxiety and insecurity of a new presiding officer than to be unprepared for a meeting. He becomes tense and strained rather than relaxed and spontaneous. Since you know that a successful meeting will depend upon appropriate seating, that announcements will need to be made, that there are always hymns to be sung and prayers to be given, see to it that these are arranged well in advance of the meeting.

2. *Be seated on the stand five minutes before the meeting commences*—This will afford you a moment to meditate and reflect on appropriate remarks to welcome the audience.

3. *Start the meeting on time*—Somehow leaders get the notion that people are "going to be late anyway," so it doesn't make any difference if the meeting is started a few minutes late. In reality it's been observed that the leadership trains people to be latecomers when the meetings are not started punctually. When members learn that meetings begin on time, the tardy problem is resolved.

4. *Make the welcome brief and appropriate*—A welcome that mentions the "beautiful weather" and profusely thanks the audience for their attendance, appears to the members to be strained and inappropriate. It would be better to say, "It's a privilege to welcome you this evening brothers and sisters to our Sacrament meeting where we have the opportunity to renew our covenants with our Father in heaven. We trust that you will add to your understanding of the

"The most delicate, the most sensible of all pleasures consists in promoting the welfare of others."

gospel and leave the meeting this evening spiritually filled. We will commence this service by singing hymn ______, after which the invocation will be offered by Brother______."

5. *Restrict lengthy announcements*—As previously mentioned, the announcements might be curtailed by having them printed in the program. The officer conducting then may need only to call attention to them, and make brief, appropriate comments after the welcome.

6. *Point out the dignity of the Sacrament*—After the invocation, the officer conducting should once again emphasize the primary purpose of the meeting. If it is a Sacrament meeting, he might say, "It's now our privilege to partake of the Sacrament in commemoration of the atonement of the Savior. As the sacramental hymn is sung, and as the bread and water are blessed and passed, let your thoughts be turned to the life and mission of the Savior and to the importance of the covenants which we are renewing. Let's turn to page ____and sing the hymn, "He Died, the Great Redeemer Died."

7. *Use proper terminology in conducting*—The prayers given to open and close the meeting should be designated, both in printed form and by way of announcement over the pulpit as the "invocation" and "benediction" respectively. The songs should be referred to as "hymns." Titled Melchizedek Priesthood bearers should be referred to as "brother" "president" "bishop" or "elder." When addressing the ward membership the congregation should be referred to as "brothers" and "sisters."

8. *Express appreciation, then close the meeting*—After the speakers have concluded their messages, it is not considered appropriate or good conducting etiquette

"He that gives all, though but little gives much; because God looks not to the quantity of the gift, but to the quality of the giver."

to comment on the messages. The only exception to this would be for the presiding officer to clarify doctrinal points that might be misunderstood or out of order. In closing the meeting the officer conducting should briefly express appreciation to those who spoke, provided special musical numbers, and the priesthood for administering and passing the Sacrament. He should then announce the closing hymn and the benediction. When these are offered, no further announcements need be given.

How do you react to the following statement:

"The most important factor in making meetings more effective is not in the technique or group participation, but the attitude of the individual toward improvement in making the presentation."

1. I accept this statement. (See below.)
2. The statement places too much stress on one individual rather than the shared responsibility of the other participants. (Turn to page 215.)

Did you say, "I accept the statement"?

I would agree! While the success of any program is due to the shared participation of all those involved, one person must be responsible for the assignment. Techniques and methods will help make the presentation more effective and interesting, but in the final analysis it is up to YOU whether a program will succeed or not. (Turn to page 223.)

Did you say, "The statement places too much stress on one individual rather than the shared responsibility of the other participants"?

While your answer is partially correct, it leaves the impression that if things don't go well, you can shift the responsibility to "the others." Actually, it's your job to see that their performance will meet a minimum acceptable standard. Whether you are willing to do this or not depends upon your present attitude toward improving the program or taking a chance on its success. (Please return to page 213 and select the other alternative.)

CHAPTER 5 SELF-TEST

1. IF you desire to get the maximum benefit from this chapter, try this exercise. Take a pencil and paper and write down a complete agenda of your organization for a future meeting. (If you are not the leader of the organization, do it anyway for the practice.) (Page 187.)

2. Given the following meetings or activities in the Church, which of the steps would be the most appropriate in making preparation for the planned activity or event. Place the numbers in back of the event.

   A. A stake dance
   B. A Sacrament meeting
   C. A Sunday School preparation meeting
   D. An MIA social
   E. A quorum cottage meeting
   F. A Relief Society dinner
   G. A Primary parade

   (See page 219 for answers.)

   1. Publish a program
   2. Make preparation for personal comfort
   3. Set a spiritual tone
   4. Prepare aids
   5. Rehearsals
   6. Checklists
   7. Spiritual preparation
   8. Contact those on the program

3. While you've got your pencil and paper handy, write down one suggestion you can use to improve any presentation you are asked to give by others; do the same with meetings you may be called upon to conduct. (Page 195.)

SELF-TEST ANSWERS

A. A stake dance	1, 2, 6, 7, and possibly 8
B. A Sacrament meeting	1, 2, 7, 8
C. A Sunday School preparation meeting	2, 4, 7, 8
D. An MIA social	2, 3, 6, 7, and possibly 8
E. A quorum cottage meeting	2, 3, 7, 8
F. A Relief Society dinner	2, 3, 4, 6, and possibly 8
G. A Primary parade	5, 6, 7, 8

Chapter 6

WANTED
THE MAN WHO IS SKILLED IN HIS ASSIGNMENT

At the completion of this chapter you should be able to:

1. LIST WHAT YOU CAN DO TO OBTAIN MORE SELF-CONFIDENCE IN YOUR ASSIGNMENT.
2. OUTLINE WHAT YOU CAN DO TO GAIN MORE SKILL IN YOUR ASSIGNMENT.
3. DESCRIBE, IN TERMS OF YOUR PRESENT ASSIGNMENT, WHAT YOU CAN DO TO BECOME MORE DEDICATED.

Chapter 6

THE MAN WHO IS SKILLED IN HIS ASSIGNMENT

What Makes a Man Skilled in His Assignment

As the stake leadership meeting adjourned, and George Hawkins hurried to his car, his soul was filled to overflowing. He could hardly wait to get home to share with Peggy the spirit of the meeting. What a tremendous leader that President Simmons is, he thought!

Since becoming a member of the ward bishopric five months ago, George had had the privilege of attending the monthly meeting with the stake presidency and other bishoprics in the stake. Since the first one he had attended, this meeting had been the most spiritually rewarding. He felt so inspired to go back to the ward to do his responsibility with greater diligence. The reason was obvious. It was the overwhelming magnitude of the Stake President, President Simmons.

As George slipped behind the wheel of his car, and quietly eased it into the northbound lane of traffic, he tried to analyze the things that made President Simmons such a magnetic leader. It wasn't his personality particularly. There were others of the brethren who seemed to stand out more in this area. It didn't seem to be his sense of humor, even though it was keen. No,

Brother Wood was a cattle rancher in Arizona. He enjoyed his work immensely, especially riding with the herd on the open range. He also served as a counselor in the stake presidency, having accepted that assignment only when the stake president promised him that he could do all of the leg work, and thus be relieved of some of the speaking assignments. Brother Wood did not consider himself talented as a speaker, and refused many of the opportunities to speak.

One evening, as Brother Wood arrived at his home, his wife informed him that a member of the First Presidency had been trying to reach him by phone, and had left a message for him to return the call. Fear and anxiety gripped him. He couldn't imagine what the First Presidency wanted with him. He realized that whatever it was it would probably involve executive talent or speaking ability. So great was his concern he didn't even stop to eat his dinner, but immediately got on his horse and rode back out on the range, where he could be alone with his thoughts and his Heavenly Father. He prayed that if it was a mission call, the Lord would change his mind. He told the Lord that he wasn't any preacher, and that he was happy with the assignment he had. He concluded his prayer however, with a willing desire to do the Lord's will. Some time later he rode back home and called Salt Lake City. It was as he had feared. He was being called on a mission, not only as a missionary but as a presiding officer —to be a mission president.

When he arrived in the mission field, his first public address contained the following: "Now I want you folks to know I ain't no preacher, I'm a Cowboy."

One year and some 200 talks later, his speaking ability had improved tremendously. Doing had made him confident. Now he spoke with authority, and like Moses, Isaiah and Elijah of old, the Lord had made him equal to the assignment, and had improved him in his area of weakness.

there seemed to be something else! Perhaps it was the abiding confidence he displayed. He always seemed to know exactly where he was going. Perhaps it was the confidence he placed in others. He seemed always to have the greatest respect and admiration, not only for the General Authorities, but for every member in the stake, particularly the bishops, with whom he counseled often. There was no doubt that President Simmons was truly a skilled leader, and George was determined that he too would become skilled in his own assignment by trying to emulate some of the qualities which President Simmons possessed.

As soon as he arrived home, he quickly wrote down the qualities he had observed in President Simmons which he felt made the president such an effective leader. They were:

1. He possesses self-confidence.
2. He is proficient at what he does.
3. He is dedicated to the Lord.

How to Develop Confidence

Throughout the millenniums of church history, one of the frequent laments of leaders chosen of the Lord is a feeling of inadequacy in their responsibilities. Enoch said, ". . . Why is it that I have found favor in thy sight, and am but a lad, and all the people hate me; for I am slow of speech; wherefore am I thy servant?" (Moses 6:31.) Moses complained similarly, ". . . O My Lord, I am not eloquent . . . but I am slow of speech, and of a slow tongue." (Ex. 4:10.) Isaiah, the eloquent statesman, deplored his call by saying, ". . . Woe is me! . . . because I am a man of unclean lips." (Isaiah 6:5.) Jeremiah hesitated with these words, ". . . Ah, Lord

"I believe the first test of a truly great man is his humility."

—Ruskin

God! behold, I cannot speak: for I am a child." (Jeremiah 1:6.) Joseph Smith declared ". . . I am not learned." (Isaiah 29:12.)

In comparing themselves against a greater standard, is it any wonder that today when an elder is called to an assignment, he is heard to say, "Why me? I'm not half as qualified for the job as Brother______ or Brother ______. Why don't you call one of them?"

The fact is that each person called to leadership opportunity may *gain* the confidence to do his assignment if three important points are remembered.

1. *The Lord calls whom he will.*—Most feel inadequate when called to a new position. The Lord knows and understands our concern but because of a pre-mortal life with him, he is aware of the potential capacity we have to do the required job. We should remember then, that the call would not have been extended if we did not have the capability to do what is expected. Reason may not justify the call in one's present state, but a realization that the Lord has been the selector should give one the confidence to accept.

Sister Banning had recently been sustained as a counselor in the Primary when she asked for an appointment to see the bishop in his office. "Bishop, I'm afraid I'm not going to be a very good person for the job." "What seems to be the problem?" he asked. "Well as you know, my responsibility is to work with the teachers, helping and advising them. I've never been a very good teacher myself. I always used to memorize the lesson word for word each time I taught. I'm not an effective teacher so how can I help others be good teachers? Frankly, I'm afraid to give suggestions because the other women surely know more about what I'm supposed to do than I do myself. What should I do, bishop?"

"Sister Banning, when you first were married, how much did you know about cooking?" "Not an awfully lot, but my mother had taught me a little," she replied. "Did this make you afraid to get married?" "No!" "Why not?" "Because I loved my husband, and I knew I could learn to cook and do other things a wife should." "Sister Banning, did you ever burn anything, or ever have a cake fall? You don't have to answer that." "Yes of course I made some mistakes." "Working in the Church is a lot like what you experienced during your first few years of married life. Just as your husband didn't expect you to be a perfect cook and homemaker, neither does the Lord, nor the teachers you direct, expect you to be a perfect leader immediately. You'll make mistakes in this work just as you did, and maybe occasionally still do, in your cooking. But just as the love for your husband helped you to try again and again, so the love you have for the Lord and the gospel will help you progress toward complete success in this calling. The Lord calls us to positions which will help us grow by struggle. Anything we do becomes boring if it is too easy, and that is why the Lord has challenged you to fill this position."

"Do you really think I can? I feel so inadequate."

2. *We are inadequate when we stand alone*—When a person is called to a position of responsibility he is not expected to stand alone. I remember while playing professional baseball, that the most basic lesson a young ball player had to learn, if he was to succeed, was to work with others. It was a natural inclination for most young players who had achieved limited success in high school or college, to want to be the "star" and stand alone. I recall the counsel of an "old" professional coach given to a group of new recruits during spring training: "Many of you think you're going to walk out on that ball diamond and play the hero. I want it understood right now that we want no individual heroes on this ball club. Winning games is a team effort. You'll be expected from this day on to play together as a single unit and the first man who tries to 'go it alone' will be benched."

Working with people in the Church is comparable to playing in athletics. Success is dependent upon team effort. The Lord, at the head, has counseled repeatedly that we cannot function adequately without his Spirit. "And the Spirit shall be given unto you by the prayer of faith; and if ye receive not the Spirit ye shall not teach." (D. & C. 42:14.) "And ye are to be taught from on high. Sanctify yourselves and ye shall be endowed with power, that ye may give even as I have spoken." (D. & C. 43:16.) Further, as we capitalize on the special talents and abilities of those assigned over us and those who work with us, confidence is gained in accomplishing the assignment.

3. *We become more confident when we understand our duty.*—Many people fall short in their church assignment because they simply do not know what to do, or what is expected of them. For example: Bob Brown, a senior member of the Aaronic Priesthood, who had recently been reactivated in the Church, was called by his bishop to the position of explorer leader in the ward.

"The Lord, your bishop, and your ward membership feel you can. You know, you're not alone—everyone in the Church holding any position feels fearful to a degree, and feels more or less inadequate. But if you couldn't fill the position, the Lord would not have called you. You were called under inspiration."

If you were to start out on an automobile trip designed to take you into various parts of your country, you would rely heavily upon a roadmap to use in plotting your journey. If you were to foolishly begin your journey without first carefully planning your course with the aid of roadmaps, travel brochures, and similar literature, your trip would be a frustrating one. You would find yourself in many difficult situations, some which would cause discouragement and loss of time. Most assuredly you would find yourself, at some point along the line, on a lonely road with your automobile out of gas. This story has a parallel in church work.

The *Instructor Magazine* (the monthly Sunday School Periodical) has a section called "The Question Box," which answers questions sent in by Sunday School teachers and leaders. Quite often the questions asked are answered by referring the inquirers to the leader's section of the Sunday School Manual, where the answer is given. Had the person submitting the question "checked his roadmap" the answer would have been found without delay and thus saved time and energy for many. Too often leaders start out on their leadership "journey" without first studying the "roadmap" provided for them. The result—somewhere along the line they get lost, start running in circles, or run out of gas.

Bob had a large family, consisting of a number of boys, and the MIA superintendent knew that he would make an excellent explorer leader. Bob was called and accepted the assignment. No instructions, manual, job description, or training experience were given to him.

One Tuesday slipped by, then two, and finally three, and Bob had only attended one of his meetings. The superintendent became alarmed, and began to wonder why he was not fulfilling his responsibility. He considered releasing Bob before he had begun. The fact was, Bob really didn't know where he was supposed to be on Tuesday night, nor what was expected of him. Whose responsibility was it to see that he understood his assignment?

a. The person issuing the call (in this case the bishop), had the responsibility and certainly the obligation to explain the assignment to him and assure him that training and integration would follow and then see that the superintendent was duly notified. As was previously discussed, this should be done at a time and place where sufficient care can be taken to ensure that the person knows exactly what is expected.

b. The recipient of the call (in this case Bob), also is obligated to *learn* his assignment. In the Doctrine and Covenants the Lord says, "Wherefore, now let every man learn his duty, and to act in the office in which he is appointed in all diligence . . . he that learns not his duty and shows himself not approved shall not be counted worthy to stand." (D. & C. 107:99-100.) The Lord, in this revelation, places the responsibility directly on the one who is called. Even though Bob may not have been familiar with this passage of scripture, he should have taken the initiative to find out the particulars of his assignment.

Misunderstanding should be problems, not tragedies.

Power comes with knowledge, understanding and wisdom.

"There is no all at once."

So the responsibility in part, belongs to Bob, but how can he come to understand his assignment? What must he do? Here are three suggestions:

1. He should arrange for a meeting where questions can be asked and discussed, instructions given, and arrangements made for brief training sessions if necessary.

2. He could confer with others who hold similar assignments in other branches or wards in the stake.

3. He should make the manual or handbook his basic tool. The handbook has been printed for the purpose of helping avert serious problem situations which could otherwise occur without knowledge or previous experience. It has further been provided to give the accumulated experiences of thousands of leaders throughout the Church in meeting the challenges of similar assignments. Well might the chemistry student disregard all the knowledge accumulated over the centuries, as for the church worker to disregard the handbook or manual.

A shy sister knew that President McKay had asked each member of the Church to "be a missionary." She thought to herself, "How can I, who am too shy to speak to my own ward members, contact an outsider and introduce him to the gospel?"

Which of the following best illustrates how she can gain the confidence to accomplish the challenge?

1. She should disregard the request in her situation since not all people are suited for such a task! (Turn to page 235.)

2. She could take her problem to the Lord and seek

"Every failure teaches a man something if he will learn."

—Charles Dickens

Asked what helped him over the great obstacles of life, a successful man answered, "The other obstacles."

"Welcome the task that makes you go beyond yourself, for then you grow."

—Louisa Y. Robinson

his help and thereby gain the confidence necessary to accomplish the challenge. (See below.)

Did you say, "She should disregard the request in her situation since not all people are suited for such a task"?

This answer is "correct"—provided you don't accept the following promise of the Lord to us when we encounter a task that is seemingly impossible to achieve:

> . . . I know that the Lord giveth no commandments unto the children of men, save he shall prepare a way for them that they may accomplish the thing which he commandeth them. (1 Ne. 3:7.)

If you do accept this counsel, please return to page 233 and select the other alternative.

Did you say, "She could take her problem to the Lord and seek his help and thereby gain the confidence necessary to accomplish the challenge"?

This is exactly what was done by this good sister. She went home and retired to her room where she poured out her concern to the Lord, explaining her feelings of inadequacy. The next day she was having lunch with a nonmember friend. It occurred to her as they were talking that they had known each other for over 20 years and yet she had never mentioned the Church to her. After a period of time, she finally mustered up the courage to ask, "What church do you attend?" Her friend responded. Then she said, "Did you know that I am a member of the Church of Jesus Christ of Latter-day Saints?" "Yes, I did," came the reply, "and ever

Heaven never helps the man who will not act.

Nature gave man two ends—one to sit on and one to think with. A man's success or failure depends on the one he uses most.

"People don't fail due to lack of knowledge but rather because they fail to use the knowledge they have. Applied knowledge is the knowledge that pays off. Application is the key. We are dealing with mortals—people who are personalities. It is important that we adapt our special knowledge and become aware of what is successful in our own experiences. There is no one best way for all men. There may however be a highly successful method for you—add your individual touch, create your own image, *see yourself.*"

since I found out you were a Mormon, I've wondered about your church because of the kind of person you are." When this shy sister recovered from her amazement she asked, "Would you be interested in learning more about my faith?" Her friend told her she would. She was later baptized a member of the Church. Since that meeting, over 100 people have become members of the Church because of this sister's influence in placing them in contact with the missionaries. And all because a shy sister, who couldn't even speak to her own ward members, had the faith to bring her problem before the Lord.

How Do I Become Proficient In My Assignment?

"There are dozens of rules for success," someone has suggested, "but none of them work unless you do." There is much to this statement because, frequently, we become our own greatest barrier.

The capacity, in other words, is within us, but what we do with our potential depends on each individual. This principle is one of the greatest in the gospel, and by keeping it foremost in our minds, it will help lead us in the direction we want to go.

One of the great educators of our time advocated a philosophy that later gave birth to the phrase, "We learn by doing." This seems consonant with the admonition of the Lord to "act" in the office to which we are called in all diligence. (D. & C. 107:99.) There simply is no substitute for experience. Reading and studying all the books in the world concerning a particular subject will never give a person what can be learned in a short time in actually doing the work. We have all heard the missionary relate how he felt he was

Quality isn't accidental, it is always the result of intelligent effort.

You are what you do.

. . . not what you want to do.

. . . not what you hope to do.

. . . not what you think you do.

. . . but what you are able to do and do do.

just beginning to be effective when it came time for his release. Why? He had learned the lessons and possessed through "doing" a degree of confidence and competence. He had also made mistakes and by so "doing" he learned to avoid the repetitions of his errors. We can all appreciate that the person with experience at any job is considered more productive than an inexperienced person. LeGrand Richards put it this way:

> The only way for anyone to enjoy this Church is to be active in it. I once heard an elder comment on this in a missionary meeting. He was quite a philosopher and a little slow of speech.
>
> He said something like this, "Well, I'm enjoying my work." Then he waited a few minutes and added, "You know that is all I can enjoy. I can't enjoy what I don't do." This statement made a profound impression upon me. I have realized that none of us will ever be able to enjoy that which we have not done. If we want much joy, we must perform much constructive work, for that is what will bring us joy. Whether it is preaching the gospel to those who know not the truth, or whether it is helping to train and educate the members of the Church to prepare them for more efficient service, or whether it is looking after the poor and unfortunate—whatever our work may be—we can only enjoy what we do.

If you're like most however, your reaction is something like this: "I don't mind working in an assignment, but I get scared!" Fundamentally, we all are! Taking a new assignment is very comparable to courting a girl. There is always the awkward period in which you're trying to learn the skill. When you've practiced enough, the awkward period disappears as do the feelings of uncertainty and insecurity. We might add parenthetically, that no one ever really overcomes that feeling of anxiety.

If a task is once begun
Never leave it 'til it's done.
Be it the labor great or small
Do it well or not at all.

When just a boy of 13, I asked the great ball player, Lou Gehrig, how I could overcome my fear on the ball field. He said, "Don't try Paul, fear can be a positive thing. Rather, learn to control it. It gives you that keen edge to do a job to the best of your capability." "Fear," he said, "reminds you that there is a divine source on which you must depend. You can't do it alone."

HIDE UNDER OR KNEEL AT YOUR BED?

One of the most tried and proven methods of learning how to control this fear is to practice the skill in a nonthreatening environment. This can easily be arranged during any meeting. Here is an illustration:

Let's suppose the home teachers have indicated to a priesthood leader in an oral evaluation that they "don't know what to talk about" while home teaching and they are having difficulty knowing how to give effective "challenges." The priesthood leader would naturally want to help them during the oral evaluation session, but the Priesthood Home Teaching Committee may feel that training of all home teachers is essential in these two areas.

At the next priesthood home teaching meeting, the home teachers might be invited. The bishop might then indicate to them that, through the oral evaluations

Deeds, not stones, are the true monuments of the great.

He who never does more than he is paid for never is paid more than he does.

conducted, it is evident they feel a need for training in the areas of (1) adapting a message to the particular home situation, and (2) issuing an effective challenge. The bishop may have one of the home teaching committee members conduct a simulated family situation. He might introduce it by reading a hypothetical background history of a typical family in the ward. This information should be similar to what is on the green family record and work sheet. As an example:

> Larry Green and his wife have been members of the Church only four years. They have two children—Rodney, age 6, and Bonnie, age 3. They attend their church meetings sporadically. Larry's occupation is a draftsman in a large factory. He is a member of the adult Aaronic Priesthood. His major hobby is chess. He has no present church assignment but has worked on the welfare farm. His wife, Margo, is fairly active. She is the Primary chorister. Her main interests are music and sewing. The boy, Rodney, is in his first year of school. He enjoys reading. Bonnie is in her first year of Junior Sunday School. She likes dolls and playing house. You are the newly assigned home teachers. How would you attempt to make friends with this family?

In every field of endeavor those who put their hearts in their work are the real leaders. Unless a man really loves his work and gets a kick out of it and is eager to get down to his job in the morning he will never make much of a mark for himself. Falling in love with one's job is the secret of success. Someone has truly said, "Be careful what you set your heart on for it will surely come true." Work is not drudgery to a man who loves his work—it is inspiring and joy and the hours sing a song of achievement.

Several options might be used to help the home teachers become skilled in this task.

1. Two home teachers may be called out of the audience and asked to demonstrate the manner in which they would approach this family. Several other home teachers could play the role of the parents and children. After the presentation has been completed, a discussion might be conducted and suggestions given whereby improvement could be made. As other *good* suggestions are made, they could also be demonstrated. One caution in the use of this technique: There needs to be an understanding that there should be no criticism of individuals since the purpose of this meeting is to help each home teacher improve. Some failure is *expected,* and also *accepted* in such a training session.

2. Another technique is to have two home teachers present a demonstration of how *not* to do home teaching. Then two others, or the same ones, may illustrate the better approach.

3. A third approach may be to have the home teachers form groups composed of 8 to 10 members. This small group situation would make it possible for all to be involved and change roles in this simulated situation thus "seeing with the other person's eyes." The priesthood leader might well be the discussion leader in each group. This technique may be used in every organization as a method of training the leadership in their assignments.

Which of the following would provide one with greater proficiency in his assigned duty?

1. Reading the manual and discussing it with other persons who are familiar with the assignment. (Turn to page 247.)

While managing a grocery store for my father I received a telephone call one afternoon from a 16-year-old high school boy. He was very much to the point—very polite—and radiated just enough self-confidence that I wanted to listen for a moment. He said, "Mr. Dunn, you don't know me. I have watched with great interest the opening of your fine market in our community. My mother has been a constant shopper there ever since, and she is delighted!" I don't know how delighted she was, but I was ready to hear more. He went on, "I realize that you probably have all of the job positions filled, but I believe I have something that will help your business. At a time that is convenient to you, sir, I would like to present my credentials. May I have an appointment?"

"How about Wednesday afternoon after school?" I asked.

"Yes sir, I can be there."

So I set it for four o'clock. At one minute to four here came the young man—smiling, properly dressed, and his step radiated confidence, but I am sure he was scared to death. As we walked into the office I had him take a seat and I pulled up a chair beside him. I said, "Tell me a little about yourself." He said, "I have had one job as a box boy on Saturdays. I believe that I know enough of the business to be an asset to your organization. Mr. Dunn, I don't expect you to hire me here and now, but I do have something your store needs." I said, "Oh, what's that?" He said, "Service! May we step into the store for just a moment?" I said, "Why, certainly." We did, and he took me over to the wall where all the canned goods were lined up. He said, "Now, Mr. Dunn, I think you know enough about sales appeal and the intuition of women as they shop to realize that if that shelf could always look full and properly aligned you could increase your sales. I'm one

2. Reading the manual, then working at the task. (See below.)

Did you say, "reading the manual and discussing it with other persons who are familiar with the assignment" would provide one with greater proficiency at the job?

Reading the manual and consulting others are certainly important if the work is to be performed according to prescribed procedures. Many studies have shown however, that on-the-job experience is the factor that leads to the greatest proficiency.

(Please return to page 245 and select the other alternative.)

Did you say "reading the manual, then working at the task" would produce greater proficiency?

You are absolutely right! Many studies have been done to show that both of these requisites are essential.

As a young boy, I read everything I could get my hands on about baseball. Reading, however, gave me no proficiency at pitching. It was the actual experience of throwing the ball toward a target that provided this skill.

How can I Become more Dedicated?

Early in the restoration of the Church, a revelation was given that cited the most important qualification for those desiring to "embark in the service of God." The of the best stock clerks in the world. I don't expect you to believe it. You even look a little doubtful. Would you be willing to let me invest one week of my time every afternoon after school to show you what I can do? And you have no obligation to pay me."

What do you imagine I was thinking? At the time I had five part-time box boys. They were more concerned about how much they were to be paid than they were about what they could give to a business. They had the capacity, but they lacked the will to serve and to give of themselves.

Do I have to tell you what I did? He worked that one afternoon. I didn't need to watch him very long. I let three boys go the next Saturday because this young man could fill all three positions.

revelation admonished "serve him [the Lord] with all your heart, might, mind, and strength." (D. & C. 4:2.)

One of the saddest of all things, is a person who has the talent and capability to render great service, but who lacks the dedication to do so. The difference between greatness and mediocrity in any man lies in either his willingness or unwillingness to give himself in service to his fellow beings. It was Voltaire who said, "I know of no great men except those who have rendered great service to the human race." What constitutes "great service" to one's fellow men?

1. *The individual possesses a capacity to care for his fellow men.*—In the nobel peace prize novel, *Dr. Zhivago,* Boris Pasternak represents the hero as saying, "Love of one's neighbor is the supreme force of vital energy. Once it fills the heart of man it has to overflow and spend itself." Such it is with dedicated men in the Church. I am impressed with the dedication and sacrifice of Latter-day Saints throughout the stakes and missions. When appreciation is extended to them on behalf of the Prophet, they invariably remark, "I appreciate the privilege to serve because it gives me the opportunity to do something for those for whom I care so much."

In New York Harbor between Manhattan and Staten Island is a sunken sheal called Robin's Reef. A small lighthouse stands there to warn of hidden dangers to those who go by sea. For many years the keeper to the Robin's Reef lighthouse has been an elderly widow by the name of Mrs. Jacob Walker. Mrs. Walker was recently interviewed by some newspapermen. She told them a story of inspiration and devotion—the story of her life.

She said: "I was a young girl living at Sandy Hook, New Jersey, when I first met Jacob Walker. He was a keeper of the Sandy Hook lighthouse. He took me there as his bride and we were very happy. Some years later we were transferred to the lighthouse at Robin's Reef. After four years my husband caught a cold while tending the light. This cold turned to pneumonia and they took him to a hospital on Staten Island. I remained behind to look after the light. A few nights later I saw a row boat coming through the darkness. Something told me the message it was bringing. We buried my husband two days later on the hillside of Staten Island not too far away to be seen from the lighthouse. Every morning since then when the sun comes up, I stand at the porthole and look across the water to Jacob's grave. Sometimes the hill is green, sometimes it is brown, sometimes it is white with snow, but I always get a message from him. It is the same thing I heard him say more often than anything else in life. It is always the same, just three words: 'Mind the light.' "

2. *The individual has a conviction that his task is truly important.*—This, of course, does not mean a patriotism to his organization to the exclusion of the importance of other church jobs, but it does mean that the individual has received a witness for himself, through prayer and devotion to his duty, that his job is singularly important to helping the total organization function. When we get this kind of conviction from a home teacher, a scoutmaster, a Primary worker, miracles begin to happen in that organization.

3. *The individual is willing to put the Lord's work first.*—Every church worker has the experience of choosing between the things he would like to do by way of personal pleasure, and doing the things he should do by way of church duty. Too often we take pride in referring to the past history of the Church in citing examples of courage and valiance in the face of opposition. We ask ourselves, "When will our 'test' come? When will we have trials similar to the pioneers?" It is my conviction that today is one of the greatest "testing" periods of all time with one of the most important tests being—to do that which we know to be our duty.

One brother who just finished his doctoral degree at a leading university—while also serving as a counselor to the bishop—gave this parting counsel to the ward membership: "I attribute the passing of my doctoral orals to one thing—putting the Lord first. I told him if he would help me through school, I would always put his work first. Over the last two years I've done my best to live up to my part of the bargain, and I want to witness to you, that if you will do this, he will help you beyond your own abilities."

4. *The individual has a realisitic goal in view.*—It's a well-known principle of psychology, that people work best when they are motivated toward a specific goal. In traveling throughout the stakes, one of the questions

Leaders need conviction. They also need to be deeply committed to their callings, to see purpose and meaning in what they do. Under the fire of conviction, fears melt away. This is illustrated in the life of Peter who, before receiving the Holy Ghost, denied his Master three times. Afterwards neither multitudes nor prison walls could hold him. The Spirit brought understanding and commitment.

Every leader should consider well his calling, see its purpose and value in the gospel plan, sense its significance in the lives of people, and commit himself to it. When this is done in faith and in trust, fear will diminish and the power of God will come into his life and strengthen him in his calling. Beautiful are the promises contained in modern revelation:

> And if your eye be single to my glory, your whole bodies shall be filled with light, and there shall be no darkness in you; and that body which is filled with light comprehendeth all things. Therefore, sanctify yourselves that your minds become single to God.
>
> —D & C 88:67-68

> Wherefore, lift up your hearts and rejoice, and gird up your loins, and take upon you my whole armor, that ye may be able to withstand the evil day, having done all, that ye may be able to stand.
>
> —D & C 27:15

> Learn of me, and listen to my words; walk in the meekness of my Spirit, and you shall have peace in me.
>
> —D & C 19:23

we frequently ask is, "What are you trying to accomplish in your organization?" There isn't one out of a hundred that has a specific, well-defined goal in mind with reference to his assignment. How does one arrive at a specific goal?

a. Most of our organizational manuals carry specific goals which are to be accomplished. These should be carefully studied, and adopted into the framework of *your* personal approach.

b. Where goals affect an organization, and no specific ones are outlined, there should be some representation by members of that organization in forming the goals. They should be very specific to be meaningful.

c. A written specific goal in terms of your personal assignment should be made. Goals, however, without a designated completion date are usually ineffectual. Therefore it is recommended that you designate a specific date in which you are to accomplish the goal. If it isn't fulfilled, you need to reassess the goal in terms of its realism; then state a goal that is more realistic. When completed, you should develop a new goal and set another completion date.

   Here are several examples of *specific* goals:

   "At the end of six months time, Rodney and John are to be fully active in the quorum."

   "At the end of this month an improvement in the reverence should be noticeable in the way our membership responds to the meetings presented."

   "At the end of three months, our home teaching should show improvement by 25 percent more challenges."

While visiting a stake conference in Idaho, I became acquainted with a young elder who was assigned to be chairman of the Fact-Finding Committee for his elders quorum. This young man took a particular pride in his assignment; not in himself, but in his assignment. He thought that it was the most important job in the whole Church. And I believe it was, because he thought so. Inside of a year, he brought that quorum from 20 percent to 85 percent activity among its members. He had truly captured the vision of the importance of his assignment.

—Marion D. Hanks

It was Saturday, the day Milt Rowley had been looking forward to all week long. As a member of the building committee for the new chapel, his nights had been pretty well spent this past week, helping to prepare the forms for the foundation. But now, it was Saturday, and he had promised the family a fishing trip to nearby Lake Suzanne. Already Mark and Tim had loaded the car, even though Mother had not as yet finished preparing breakfast.

Above the muffled shouts and boasts of who was to have the greatest success that day, Milt heard the phone ringing. He hurried to the bedroom extension, and wiping the shaving cream from around one ear, picked it up. A voice said, "Milt, this is the bishop calling. The cement trucks are here to pour concrete this morning, and we need your help. Don Jacobs was supposed to be here this morning, but he called to apologize, stating that he suffered a bad ankle sprain in last night's game, and just can't walk this morning. We really need you. You will come won't you?"

What would you do?

1. I would go with my family on this fishing trip feeling that I could not disappoint them at this time. (See below.)
2. I would tell the bishop of my willingness to go, and then request that the family join me on the project. (Turn to Page 257.)

Did you say, "I would go with my family on this fishing trip feeling I could not disappoint them at this time"?

This would certainly be an excusable approach under the circumstances! In doing so, however, a great teaching experience for the boys might well have been by-

Sister Matthews entered her classroom that first day with excitement. She had never been given an assignment to teach young teen-agers before, and she sincerely hoped she could make this Sunday School experience a rich one for the 17 students assigned to her class. She realized the importance of the assignment. Had not the bishop told her that these years were the golden years for youth? It was at this time in their lives when they made some of the big decisions, such as whether to continue in church activity or fall away into inactivity. How she prayed that she could reach their hearts with the spirit of the gospel.

As these young people entered the room, Sister Matthews greeted each warmly, and maintained the same friendliness throughout the lesson. She had prepared well, and everything seemed to be running smoothly as she tried to involve each one. Oh there was some whispering, shuffeling and giggling going on, but the students responded well to the lesson. The thing which bothered Sister Matthews most was that only 12 of the 17 were in Sunday School that day.

After class, Sister Matthews looked over the roll book and wrote down the names of the five that were missing that day. She knew that unless those boys and girls came to Sunday School, they would miss much, and their entire lives might be affected. So, during the week, she visited the homes of each of the five, after clearing with the individual's home teacher, and personally invited each one to Sunday School. Success was not immediate, but as she continued to contact and get better acquainted with those who were absent, they all began coming to her class. Some would come occasionally, and then regularly. She made sure that they would want to come, by preparing and giving her lessons with study, prayer, and diligence.

passed. They undoubtedly would have learned through a dad's example what devotion to duty means, what the priesthood means to him. To find out what happened in this situation, please see alternate answer.

Did you say, "I would tell the bishop of my willingness to go, and then request that the family join me on the project"?

This is what this brother did! The story continues:

Milt responded, "Yes bishop, you can count on me being there." He then called the family together and told them of the bishop's desire. He said, "I've told the bishop he could call on me any time he needed my help. I know this is a terrific disappointment to all of us, but I can't let him down." The boys complained, "Why do we always get called upon, Dad?" "I feel boys, that this is the finest compliment that can be given to a priesthood bearer—to be called upon. I know this is a disappointment to you, but why can't we all go over to the chapel, put in a day's work, and go out together this evening to a movie, or whatever you want to do." The family agreed, with the result that they not only did something together, but felt good that they had fulfilled their responsibility. (Turn to page 263.)

Eventually her dedication paid off, as her students began to attend other meetings as well. It wasn't too many years until the first of her class had his mission farewell. She was so proud of Jay that night, as he stood to bear testimony of the truth, and to pay honor to a little lady that had helped him appreciate the importance of living the gospel.

Sister Matthews had obtained the goal she sought—all 17 of those assigned her were in the fold.

CHAPTER 6 SELF-TEST

1. List at least one thing you can do to become more confident in your church assignment. (Page 225.)
2. Describe briefly how you or another person, who holds a difficult assignment, may become more skilled at the task. (Page 237.)
3. Indicate what you desire to do to become more dedicated in your church responsibility. (Page 247.)

Chapter 7

THE MAN WHO CAN EFFECTIVELY COUNSEL OTHERS

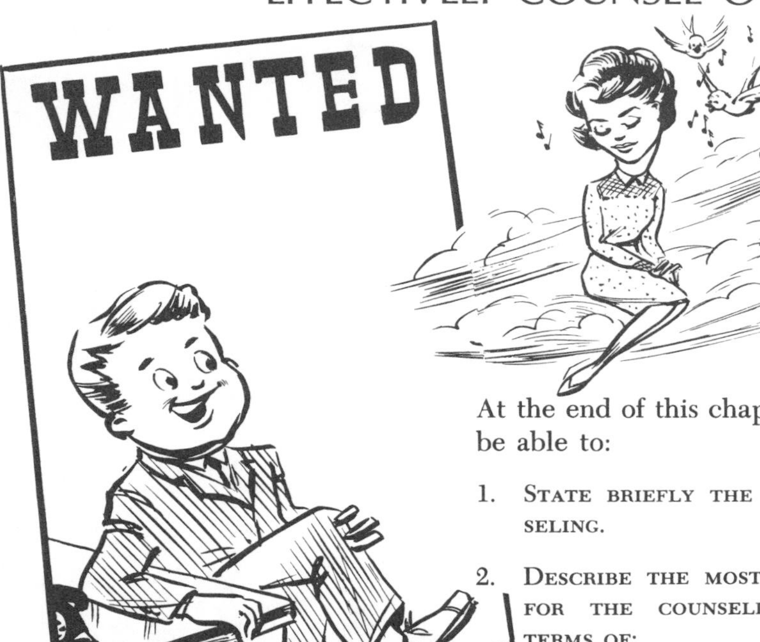

At the end of this chapter you should be be able to:

1. State briefly the purpose of counseling.
2. Describe the most ideal conditions for the counseling interview in terms of:
   - a. where and when to counsel,
   - b. how long to counsel in an interview and,
   - c. what the most desirable seating arrangement would be.
3. Relate how you can improve your own counseling techniques and methods in the following areas:
   - a. establishing a relationship of trust and concern for another person,
   - b. getting the other person to talk about his real problem,
   - c. teaching the other person to solve his problems through reliance on his divine resources.

Chapter 7

THE MAN WHO CAN EFFECTIVELY COUNSEL OTHERS

Why Do We Counsel Others?

In Chapter three some of the causes of human behavior were discussed. It was pointed out that the behavior of a person arises out of the needs and wants he desires to satisfy. While the physical needs are worthy, others are equally valid and are what we might refer to as social or "tempted needs," those which prevent the person from realizing his higher spiritual potential. When people seek guidance or help, it must be remembered that their action or behavior is an honest attempt to satisfy these needs, either worthy or tempted.

Why then do we counsel? Many reasons could be cited but two are most relevant:

1. We are attempting to TEACH the person to satisfy his needs in a way that will provide the greatest happiness to him as an individual.

2. We are attempting to assist him to stand alone; to eventually get along without counsel. In other words, the fact that we teach a person the process by which he can gain greater happiness, should also enable him to act with greater independence once he knows how to apply his own insights and resources in solving a problem.

WHAT COUNSELING IS:

1. Counseling is a relationship between two people, one of whom seeks help from another.
2. Counseling is giving understanding and respect to another person's problem.
3. Counseling is thinking *with, not for,* the other person.
4. Counseling is helping the other person to become independent of your help.
5. Counseling is acceptance of another person as an individual of worth, of divine potential.
6. Counseling is treating all information given to you in a confidential manner.
7. Counseling is understanding human nature and the reasons for the behavior of people.

WHAT COUNSELING IS NOT:

1. Counseling is *NOT* giving advice.
2. Counseling is *NOT* lecturing another to conform.
3. Counseling is *NOT* judgment over the other person.

What are the Most Ideal Conditions for the Counseling Interview?

Where to Counsel

When an individual seeks counsel it is advisable to meet in a place that will allow maximum privacy. The reason for this is obvious. No person wants to "bare his soul" or reveal a personal problem when there is a fear of being overheard or interrupted. Therefore, it is recommended that you find an office or place where privacy can be assured.

When Do You Counsel?

The answer to this question may seem obvious, but is one of the most important considerations to effective counseling. One counsels when another asks for or is in need of help. While designating a specific time and place is important, it is more important that the counselor be available when the need is greatest and when the heart and mind of the counselee are most receptive.

There may be occasions which call for a counseling situation in which you are the instigator. The attitude and action of those working under your direction may require that you call an individual in to discuss a problem or situation. You would then call the person to come to you and confront him with the problem of which he may or may not be aware. In so doing, you will have to remember that a leader-initiated interview is not usually as effective as when the person himself asks for help, the reason being that the individual is more motivated to listen to counsel when he already recognizes he has a problem and that it is keeping him from greater self-fulfillment. People are always more receptive when they have requested the help.

Instead of this...

Try this...
Or this

What is the Best Seating Arrangement for Counseling?

Most authorities recommend that the person to be counseled sit in a face-to-face relationship with no physical barrier, such as a desk, between him and the counselor. This lack of a barrier establishes a feeling of equality and makes it possible for the counselor to give undivided attention. An across the desk interview, on the other hand, conveys "superiority" of the counselor to the counselee. It further gives the person being counseled the expectation that you will solve all his problems much the same as a medical doctor would provide you with a medical diagnosis. If your physical arrangement necessitates an around-the-desk interview, it is recommended that you use the seating arrangements as illustrated in figures 2 and 3.

How Long Should the Counseling Interview Last?

The length of the interview will depend on the nature and content of the problem, but in a usual counseling situation it should not last more than an hour. Most authorities feel that little good can be accomplished beyond this point. If further time is needed, it is best to summarize the interview at the end of 50 to 60 minutes and then suggest that the party return at a future time.

There is an advantage to having some time elapse between interviews. It allows the counselee to think over what has been said and to further evaluate his problem. Some leaders make it a practice to assign reading material that is relevant to the problem. Others ask the person to make a written evaluation of the problem with all possible solutions listed, and then return to discuss the alternatives.

TOO BUSY TO CARE?

Julia Ward Howe, author of the "Battle Hymn of the Republic," was making an impassioned plea to a politician, seeking his aid for a friend of hers who badly needed assistance. The man replied, "Julia, I've become so busy I can no longer concern myself with individual cases."

"Fortunately," replied Mrs. Howe, "God hasn't reached that stage yet!"

What would you do in the following situations? You are stopped in the church foyer by a person who anxiously asks, "May I talk to you a minute about a problem?" Which of the following best describes the most appropriate thing to do to provide the best conditions for a counseling interview?

1. Step aside to the corner of the foyer and say, "Now what can I do to help you?" (See below.)

2. Ask the person to step into an empty office or classroom with you so that you will not be interrupted. (See below.)

Did you say you would "step aside to the corner of the foyer and say, 'Now what can I do to help.' "?

This alternative may be appropriate for a situation that isn't serious, or is not a personal problem. When the person indicates that he has a problem, however, it is usually better to seek a private room where he can talk without fear of interruption. (Please check No. 2 as a possibility.)

Did you say you would "ask the person to step into an empty office or classroom with you so that you will not be interrupted"?

When you sense a problem is serious, this is the better approach since he will feel he can talk with you without fear of interruption. It is not uncommon for a leader to consent to listen to one's problems and as soon as the person steps into the office, or room, he or she bursts into tears. Such an emotional release in front of

"Now those men, or those women, who know no more about the power of God, and the influences of the Holy Spirit, than to be led entirely by another person, suspending their own understanding, and pinning their faith upon another's sleeve, will never be capable of entering into celestial glory. . . . They cannot rule themselves, to say nothing of ruling others, but they must be dictated to in every trifle, like a child. They cannot control themselves in the least, but James, Peter, or somebody else must control them. . . . They never can hold sceptres of glory, majesty, and power in the celestial kingdom. Who will? Those who are valiant and inspired with the true independence of heaven, who will go forth boldly in the service of their God, leaving others to do as they please, determined to do right, though all mankind besides should take the opposite course. Will this apply to any of you? Your own hearts can answer."

—Brigham Young, *Journal of Discourses*,
Vol. 1, page 312.

others would cause personal embarrassment. Frequently those burdened with a problem will not seek help if privacy is not assured.

How to Improve Your Counseling Technique and Method

In considering the counseling process the following steps are most important:

1. Establish a relationship of trust and concern for the individual.
2. Get the person to talk about his real problem.
3. Teach him to solve his problems through personal insight using his own resources and show how reliance upon the divine can be helpful.

This total process may take one or several sessions, depending upon the person or the nature and extent of the problem. Let's consider how you can be effective in each of these areas.

How to Establish a Relationship of Trust and Concern for People

The most important, and most difficult, phase of the counseling experience is to establish a relationship of trust and concern. As Glasser has noted, the person who comes for help

> . . . is looking for a person with whom he can become emotionally involved, someone he can care about and who he can be convinced cares about him, someone who can convince the [other person] that he will stay with him until he can better fulfill his

Two brothers convicted of stealing sheep, were branded on the forehead with the letters ST, for "Sheep Thief."

One brother, unable to bear the stigma, tried to bury himself in a foreign land, but men asked him about the strange letters. He wandered restlessly, and at length, full of bitterness, died and was buried in a forgotten grave.

The other brother said, "I can't run away from the fact that I stole sheep. I will stay here and win back the respect of my neighbors and myself."

As the years passed he built a reputation for integrity. One day a stranger saw the old man with the letters branded on his forehead. He asked a native what they signified. "It happened a great while ago," said the villager. "I've forgotten the particulars; but I think the letters are an abbreviation of Saint."

—Macartny's Illustrations,
(Abingdon-Cokesbury)

needs. (William Glasser, M.D., *Reality Therapy, A New Approach to Psychiatry,* New York, Harper and Row Publishers, 1965, p. 21.)

If the counselor fails in this phase, all else will fail too! Let's consider from the standpoint of the person who comes for help what must be done to establish a relationship of trust and concern.

1. He needs to know you are concerned with him alone, and he can sense when that concern is real or when it is feigned. This is demonstrated to him by the way you react toward him and his problem—whether you are aloof or warm, whether you are "superior," or human, brusque or sensitive.

Some of the ways effective counselors have found to show this concern is to ask at the beginning of the interview, "Tell me something about yourself—your interests, what you're doing." If not familiar with the individual and his background, you may at this point want to ask questions concerning his family, childhood, job etc. These are familiar areas to him and he feels secure in responding. It also gives him an opportunity to discern your desire to help. As he talks, you will need to be aware of areas where he indicates pride and self-esteem so that these experiences may be used by you to help him acquire more confidence in his outlook toward himself.

The most important thing a counselor can do in demonstrating concern is to listen to the other *with feeling.* By this is meant that he is intent on every expression of the other person. The counselor tries to capture the emotion or *feeling* of the other, rather than just the *content* of what he is saying. Further, he allows nothing to distract his attention from the other person—no paper shuffling, no wandering eyes, or mind on other matters.

"The best portions of a good man's life are his little, nameless, unremembered acts of kindness and love."

—Wordsworth

The other person becomes the sole focal point of his concern. There is nothing more disconcerting than to sit in the presence of one who is so preoccupied with other things that he has no interest in you.

2. He needs to have a person whom he can trust and who will accept him as a person of equal worth.

Trust and concern is the key.

Each of us lives within a realm or "world" that is distinctly our own. Even those closest to us may not come into this "world" unless by special invitation. For it is here that we harbor our dreams, ambitions, insecurities, secrets and fears. This is that part of us that reveals who we *really are,* not what we appear to be. And so we invite only those few to share this "world" who we know we can trust not to betray or reject us.

How does a counselor establish this "relationship of trust"—to be allowed to enter the other's world? It is communicated to the other by the way you listen and how you respond that you consider him to be a person of real worth. This, of course, is sometimes difficult,

Remember the worth of souls is great in the sight of God; For, behold, the Lord your Redeemer suffered death in the flesh; wherefore he suffered the pain of all men, that all men might repent and come unto him.

D. & C. 18:10-11

particularly when the other reveals a set of values that are different from your own. At times your acceptance will be tested by statements that exaggerate the actual behavior. Recognizing that people do not make behavioral changes to satisfy higher needs till the lower needs of acceptance and love are satisfied, it is absolutely essential that you follow the example of the Master by accepting the individual *where he is* before exposing him to other behavioral alternatives. As an example, you would not at this point mention the reforming of any bad habits or living in accord with the principles of the gospel. He first must know you accept him the way he is, without condemning.

You will find that your mental attitude has a great deal to do with the conveying of acceptance or rejection to the other person. A condemning, rejecting, or judgmental attitude on your part will confirm a feeling of worthlessness and dispair to him. This kind of mental attitude toward others communicates, "You should have known better," "If you had followed the commandments, this wouldn't have happened," or "Hurry and get to what's on your mind as I've a very demanding schedule to keep." Whether communicated openly or silently, the effect is the same—the individual will feel rejected by you and will not reveal his honest feelings.

The opposite attitude, one of acceptance, affirms to the individual that he is a person of worth and has within himself the divine resources to solve his problems or conquer his weaknesses. This attitude on your part communicates, "I believe in you as an individual. I believe you have what it takes to solve this problem. I hope I can be of some help to you." When this confidence is communicated to the other person, the invitation will be given to you to step inside his "world."

People need someone to experience their "world" of anxiety and suffering with them. Once trust has been

A COUNSELOR DESCRIBES EMPATHY

While he talked I sat perfectly relaxed and let my eyes rest on his face. I permitted myself to become absorbed in his story; and soon I was so completely engrossed that I was unconscious of our physical surroundings in the room and aware only of this boy's frightened eyes, his tremulous voice, and the fascinating human drama which he was describing.

He told how his father had used to beat him during his boyhood on the farm, and how he had grown up without parental love or understanding. During this moment I felt the pain of his father's beatings, curious as it may seem, as though I myself were receiving the blows. Then he told of running away to high school, where he had supported himself alone under great handicaps. Through high school he had been burdened by an overpowering sense of inferiority. And as he described this inferiority feeling, a depression occurred in myself as though the inferiority had been my own.

Then the young man spoke of his early wish to come to college, which had been met by his parents' sarcastic prediction that he would not be able to last it a semester. With bulldog determination he had nevertheless arrived on the campus, practically penniless. Since then—he was now a sophomore—he had been working his way while struggling at the same time to keep up in studies for which he was poorly prepared. Speaking then of his college experience, he described the shyness and inferiority feeling which continued to oppress him and the loneliness that he suffered even in the midst of the hurly-burly of campus life.

—Rollo May, *The Art of Counseling*, (New York, Nashville: Abingdon Press), pp. 76-77. Used by permission of Abingdon Press.

Come into my world.

established, the individual will invite you into his "world." When you share this "world" together, the relationship of trust and concern has been established. Your emotions have now become blended, and you become a part of his experience. He has now, in part, fulfilled a need through you by having someone care enough to share his anxiety and suffering.

To quote May:

> This is empathy. It is the feeling, or the thinking of one personality into another until some state of identification is achieved. In this identification, real understanding between people can take place; without it . . . no understanding is possible . . . [those] who deal intimately with persons had best endeavor to understand it, for their success depends on their ability to accomplish this walking with another person into the deepest chambers of his soul. (Rollo May, *The Art of Counseling,* Nashville: Abingdon Press, 1939, pp. 77-78.)*

When a relationship of trust and concern is established, one needs only to ask, "What can I do to help?"

*Used by permission.

THE COUNSELING APPROACH USED BY THE "WONDERFUL COUNSELOR"

His Philosophy:

1. He saw himself as having a special mission to help men realize their divine potential.

2. He saw each person as an individual of inestimable worth, notwithstanding their sins.

3. He regarded man as being the literal son of the Eternal Father thus giving the individual a divine capacity of perfection.

4. He regarded each man unique from all other men.

5. He regarded man responsible for his behavior when he understood the difference between good and evil.

6. He saw man as being both "good" and "evil." When man chose righteousness, he was "good"; when he chose unrighteousness, he was "evil."

7. He counseled that man was capable of a perfected nature which consisted of acquiring godlike attributes.

8. He counseled that the foremost barrier to man's perfection was sin. Sin produced guilt in the individual, which in turn caused feelings of unworthiness, anxiety and personality disintegration. He further taught that guilt and anxiety could be carried into the next life, if man did not repent.

9. He counseled that there were three types of sin which retarded man's progress. These were: sins of self indulgence, sins of pride, and sins of self-seeking.

or "What is it you came to tell me?" to get the person to talk about his problem.

How to Get An Individual to Talk About His Problem

There are several ways in which a person may indirectly attempt to introduce his problem. Three of the most frequently used are:

1. Referring to the problem in the third person, such as, "I have a friend that. . . ."
2. The indirect question, such as, "What happens to people who . . .?"
3. Presenting a less serious problem before introducing the real problem.

Your handling of these questions or "problems" will determine the other's willingness to go deeper into his "secrets" with you. In most cases, these questions on contrived situations are tests to determine your acceptance of him as an individual. If you condemn the "situation" or "3rd" person, chances are you will be thanked and the person will leave without being helped by you.

Your wisdom will immediately suggest to you that not every question or situation described by another is a "cover-up" for his personal problem. But how can you discern those that are from those that are not? Here are several suggestions:

1. Let's consider first the problems presented in the third person such as one where the individual asks for advice about a friend that is having marital difficulty. You might say something like this, "Well Gene, I'd

10. He further counseled that there were three conditions to realizing one's potential divinity. To overcome the sins against self-indulgence, one needs to learn self-control. To overcome the sins of pride, one needs to discover his divine worth. To overcome the sins of self-seeking, one needs to consecrate all his heart, might, mind and strength to others and the kingdom of God. All commandments were given to this end.

His Practice:

1. As a counselor, Jesus was a teacher of *the way*. He perceived that man did not have the fulness of truth to realize his potential destiny. Man, therefore, needed to be taught concerning this potential, and how it could be achieved.

2. To examine his counseling method in a relationship with one other person, you may want to investigate the following situation. Note how Jesus was able to perceive the person's problem immediately, how he counseled that individual toward self-fulfillment, and how he allowed the person the agency to make his own decision.

   a. Counseling an adulterous woman to overcome a sin of self-indulgence. (John 8:1-22.)

   b. Counseling a lawyer to overcome the sin of pride. (Luke 10:25-38.)

   c. Counseling a teacher of religion to overcome the sin of self-seeking. (John 3:1-22.)

Is it any wonder that Isaiah called him a "Wonderful Counselor"?

—William O. Nelson, unpublished paper

have to know more about the case before I could even suggest any ways to help your friend. Tell me more." (What you have just told him, is, "I don't judge a situation before learning all the facts.") As he now begins to relate the particulars of the situation, you might ask questions to clarify—but never to interject judgment or opinion at this point. When the problem has been described, but is still in the third person, that is, relating to his friend, you might comment, "I can see why you are so concerned about your friend's situation. He truly does need understanding and help." (You have told him, "I'm ready to understand your problem if you want to tell me.") In many cases, the individual states at this point, "As you might have guessed, this is Dora's and my problem," in which case you can explore with him the total area of difficulty. If, however, he still will not reveal that the person referred to is himself, and presses you, "What should I do?" you might say, "Knowing this person better than I, Gene, what solutions suggest themselves to you?" When these are offered, if they are practical, it is good practice to commend him for his suggestions of the solution to the problem, and add, "You might further consider these alternatives," to those not mentioned. By this time you will have demonstrated that he can place his confidence and trust in you without fear of condemnation.

2. The indirect question is difficult to handle because of the tendency in all of us to want to answer the question. Also, a person needing help will ask an indirect question when there is fear of embarrassment in front of others. When you sense this, it is appropriate to suggest, "Why don't you step in the office sometime and we can discuss it." When a forthright question is asked such as, "How serious do you feel adultery is?" it's usually best to say, "I think you already know what the Church teaches on that subject. I might add, however, that the door is always open to a person who

Practice blindness to other's faults, looking always for their good qualities instead.

wants to overcome such a problem." Usually at this point the person will introduce the problem as his own or will disguise it in the third person in which case the foregoing suggestions would be used.

3. An individual will frequently "test" your acceptance of him by presenting first a less serious problem than the real one that concerns him, or he may not know what the real problem is—only that he has anxiety. He may introduce the problem this way: "I'm having problems with my studying in school—got any ideas?" A normal tendency is to try to counsel him on his study habits, thus preventing him from exploring the real problem. Make sure that you know that this is the problem he wants to talk about before you give any information or answers. When he asks the question—"got any ideas?" you might say, "Tell me more about your problem—what you're doing that seems to be causing it." This will in most cases give you some clues of the source of his real difficulty.

To help a person clarify his feelings about symptoms to a problem which are not clearly evident to himself, you may find it helpful to use the following techniques:

a. Watch for emotionally toned words. For example, the person may say, "I feel *inadequate* all the time in everything I do." The word "inadequate" is his way of trying to express his feeling. To help him clarify it more, a counselor might reflect back to him, "You use the word 'inadequate', what do you mean?"

b. Get the person to describe the behavior that seems to cause his feelings of frustration and unhappiness. To illustrate: A housewife may attempt to describe a constant frustration around her husband. When she is unable to clarify, a counselor might ask, "Tell me about an average day in your home that would describe the rela-

"Lead others to your view, if you are sure you are right, by questions rather than arbitrary statements or argumentation."

tionship between you and your husband." As she describes particular things they do or say, the counselor can then ask, "How does this make you *feel* when he says this to you?" The purpose of exploring the "doing—feeling" level with the other person is to give you an indication of her needs, and whether she feels responsibility for what is happening in the home. The significance of this will be discussed in section three.

c. Another technique used is to reflect the feeling of the other person's statements. This requires a great deal of practice—but most of all empathy. The counselee might say, "I just don't know where to start—my feelings are so mixed up." The counselor might respond to this, "I understand. At times it's really hard to talk about your feelings, isn't it?" This assurance will provide the other person with the courage to explain his feeling further. A caution on the use of this technique: If it's uncomfortable to you, don't use it! A good rule of thumb to follow in any counseling situation is "when in doubt—*don't!*"

A good rule of thumb.

"The only way to have a friend is to be one."

—Emerson

THE ONLY WAY TO HAVE A FRIEND

The only way to have a friend
Is to be one yourself;
The only way to keep a friend
Is to give from that wealth.

For friendship must be doublefold,
Each one must give his share
Of feelings true if he would reap
The blessings that are there.

If you would say, "He is my friend,"
Then nothing else will do
But you must say, "I am his friend,"
And prove that fact be true.

—Author Unknown

What would you do in the following situation?

The branch president had just stepped out of his office when one of the members asked to speak with him. When they were seated in the office, she told him, "I'm having trouble with Marvin, our oldest son. He is really giving the teachers a bad time. I thought I could get some suggestions from you."

Which of the following would describe how you could best handle this situation from a counseling point of view?

1. Assure her that this is a normal boy's problem, then counsel her to try to be understanding of him as a growing boy. (See below.)
2. Ask her to tell you more about the problem and what seems to have caused his behavior to be the way it is. (See below.)

Did you say you would "assure her that this is a normal boy's problem, then counsel her to try to be understanding of him as a growing boy"?

This may be excellent advice, but it is not counseling. By having her explore the depth and extent of the problem with you, you would be in a much better position to considering alternatives to solve this problem. (Please check No. 2 as a more realistic choice.)

Did you say you would "ask her to tell you more about the problem and what seems to have caused his behavior to be the way it is"?

Try consciously to keep your feelings "in tune" with the feelings of those about you.

This approach proved best in this situation. Here is how she further described the homelife situation:

> I don't know exactly where to begin. Ever since Wendell took on that additonal night job, we have been having trouble with Marvin. His dad is the only one who can do anything with the boy, and he's never home when Marvin is, except on Sunday. "It appears," said the branch president, "that we had better include your husband in on our talk. How do you think he would respond to the possibility of our talking with him?"

As the branch president and this couple talked over the problem, the husband could see that a real problem did exist and he had been totally unaware of his contribution to it. He decided that the risk of losing his boy was not worth the extra money he was earning on another job. He quit, and almost miraculously, the boy's behavior changed.

Teaching Another to Solve Problems Using His Own Resources and Gaining Assistance from the Lord

Once the perceived problem of a person is exposed, it becomes the counselor's task to help him find new ways to fulfill his needs more satisfactorily. Change will only occur when this happens.

The experience of Jesus being tempted in the wilderness, coupled with our own observation and experience, confirms the truth that all temptation comes to man in three ways. As we understand these three temptations and how they relate to the needs of man, we are in a position to help those who seek counsel to fulfill these needs in a more satisfactory manner.

THE DIVINE THERAPY

Basic Needs and the Temptation	*The Problem Symptom*	*The Real Problem*	*The Therapy*
I. Satisfaction of the following needs through self-indulgence A. Giving and receiving love B. Acceptance C. Recognition D. Belongingness	I. Indulgence, Intemperance A. Uncontrollable temper B. Word of Wisdom Problems C. Abusive language D. Reading lewd magazines or pornographic literature E. Aggressive behavior F. Immorality	I. Lack of self-control Person has not been able to satisfy the needs of love, acceptance and recognition through healthy relationships with others, so he attempts to satisfy these needs through self-indulgence which provides temporary happiness.	I. Control Self A. Must learn to *confess* and *forsake* sin B. Must develop satisfactory relationships with people who fulfill their needs in a more satisfactory manner (Close fellowshipping in the gospel)
II. Satisfaction of the following needs through self-deception A. Acceptance by self B. Acceptance by others C. Giving and receiving love D. Recognition	II. Exaggeration or Depreciation of Self-worth A. Inferiority feelings B. Despair C. Superiority feelings D. Indecisiveness E. Exaggeration F. Sarcasm G. Gossipping H. All forms of disrespect L. Deception J. Dishonesty	II. Problem of Pride Person has attempted to satisfy the need for love, recognition, acceptance by pretending to be someone other than his true self. He finds that a feeling of insecurity constantly plagues him, so he "covers" this feeling by various "fronts."	II. Know Thyself A. Must learn to accept self and others B. Must be willing to make an honest introspection of his own worth C. Must discover through the Holy Ghost, patriarchal blessings, and help of others, his divine worth
III. Satisfaction of the following needs through self-seeking A. Prestige B. Creativity C. Making a contribution of worth D. Self-fulfillment	III. Self-advancement as an end in itself A. Seeking gain or status as an end to satisfy personal ambition B. Unwillingness to give time, talent, money to the kingdom of God C. Disrespect of Sabbath Day D. All forms of self-enhancement (Power-seeking)	III. Self-exaltation or lack of consecration. Person is attempting to satisfy his needs for prestige, recognition and self-fulfillment through seeking worldly ends which gives to him this temporary satisfaction, but he finds that he still lacks self-fulfillment.	III. "Lose Thyself" A. Needs to dedicate himself first to the upbuilding of others and the kingdom of God

The first temptation is to satisfy the need for love, belongingness and acceptance through the means of self-indulgence. When a person gives in to this temptation, we might observe one or several of the following symptoms: (1) uncontrollable temper, (2) abusive language, (3) reading lewd magazines and pornographic literature, (4) aggressive behavior, (5) immoral action, and (6) Word of Wisdom problems. The basic problem underlying these symptoms is that the individual hasn't learned to be responsible for his behavior. Self-indulgence has seemed to him to have been the most expedient way for him to satisfy his needs. It is the counselor's task to (1) get him to take the responsibility for his actions, and (2) help him to learn ways to gain self-control so that he may fulfill his immediate needs and go on to satisfy his higher needs and potential.

The second temptation is to satisfy one's needs of self-acceptance, acceptance by others, love, recognition and self-esteem through the use of deceptive "fronts" or pride. Symptoms to this problem are feelings of (1) despair, (2) inferiority, (3) superiority, (4) indecisiveness, (5) exaggeration, (6) sarcasm, (7) gossipping, (8) all forms of disrespect, (9) deception and (10) dishonesty. The real problem underlying these symptoms is a pretense to be someone we are not. It therefore becomes the responsibility of the counselor to help the individual discover his real potential and show him how to use it to fulfill these needs more satisfactorily.

The third temptation is to satisfy one's needs for recognition, prestige, making a creative contribution, and self-fulfillment through self-seeking means. Symptomatic of the attempt to meet these needs through self-oriented means are these behavior patterns: (1) seeking gain or status as an end to satisfy personal ambition, (2) unwillingness to give time, or talent, or money to the upbuilding of the kingdom, (3) disrespect of the Sabbath day, and (4) all form of self-enhancement. The

A bishop was aroused late one night by an angry member of his ward pounding on his door. He was threatening to do harm to a neighbor. The bishop tried to calm him by asking him some questions. The individual merely restated his intentions. He refused to come into the house to discuss the matter further with the bishop. The bishop went to his room, got his coat and encouraged the man to drive down to his office with him. As they rode along the bishop could feel the trembling and see the tenseness of his fellow member. His heart went out in fervent prayer seeking guidance and inspiration to solve the problem. An answer came sooner and more direct than he had ever expected. An inner voice plainly stated, "Pray with this man." The bishop had just recently completed a Ph. D. in the area of counseling and to pray with a man on the border of hysteria seemed unreasonable in light of his professional training and he dismissed the thought from his mind. After arriving at the Church and while walking down the corridor he received the same impression, "Pray with this man." As they walked into his office he turned to the man, and simply said, "Will you pray with me?" The man fell to his knees. The bishop knelt down and offered a humble prayer for guidance and inspiration and then turned to the member and asked him to pray. He poured out a confession of sin and guilt that first seemed unbelievable, but upon completion, two changed men stood facing each other. A miraculous change came over the member. His anger was gone. He was full of humility and repentance, seeking forgiveness and wanting to know the path of forgiveness and repentance.

real problem underlying these symptoms is unspirituality or worldly-mindedness. Here the counselor has the responsibility to show the other person how he can "lose himself" and find satisfaction to his higher or spiritual needs.

It must be noted at this point that any attempt by the counselor to treat the symptoms, or outward behavior, without showing the person how to fulfill his needs in a more satisfactory manner to HIM, will not result in changed behavior. How this can be done might be illustrated by taking three sample problems from the category of temptations.

1. *Working with problems of self-indulgence.*

Once a person states that he is not satisfied with his present behavior, he has in part committed himself to a new course of action. The counselor needs then to remind him of a better alternative, "You *can* do something about your problem, you know!" To this may be suggested various atlernatives. When these have been thoroughly explored, the counselor might ask, "What do you want to do about the problem?" If he chooses not to change his behavior, it may be asked, "How is this going to help you become a happier person?" If the person has no desire to change the behavior at this point, little can be done to help. If, however, he expresses a determination to do something about his problem, the counselor can now get a firm commitment that this is to be his new course of action. He might do this by saying, "Are you certain this is what you want to do? It's going to be a difficult road!" When the person has firmly committed himself to the new behavior, then the counselor needs to help him make a realistic plan of action which will enable him to attain his objective. "What are you going to do to make certain you accomplish your goal?" he may ask. "What's your first step?" It is then necessary to have the person

"A man's mind may be likened to a garden which may be intelligently cultivated or allowed to run wild; but when no useful seeds are put into it, then an abundance of useless weed seeds will fall therein and will continue to produce their kind."

return periodically and give an accounting on his progress. If he has failed, it is imperative that he be reminded of his commitment. This can only be done effectively when you have a relationship that keeps him returning because you are helping meet, perhaps for the first time, his needs of love and acceptance. If you excuse his behavior, you are in effect telling him, "I didn't have the confidence you could do it anyway." He needs to know you are a person who will never give up on him, so if he fails in his attempt, while you will understand, you don't endorse the action, but start the process over again.

What you are teaching him, without preachment or moralization, is self-control. This is the only way he will overcome the problem of self-indulgence. Once overcome, he moves onto a higher need level.

Your work, however, is not completed with the interviews. Recall that unless his need for love, belongingness and acceptance is fulfilled, he will revert to the same behavior EVEN THOUGH HE DESIRES TO CHANGE. It is at this point that you get others involved with him. If you are not his bishop, and it is the kind of problem that should be referred to his ecclesiastical leader, it might be handled this way: "In addition to our meeting together to see what might be done about your problem, I'm sure you realize that the Lord has established the way by which you can make your life whole again. As a 'judge in Israel' the Lord will bless your bishop not only in understanding you and your problem but also in assisting you to find the right solutions. Would it be all right with you if I set up an appointment?" Ofttimes members are reluctant to go to those in authority over them because either they are strangers or they feel they cannot trust their leader.

It is important also to see that the peer group of the individual is involved when appropriate. This may be

"The soul attracts that which it secretly harbors, that which it loves, and also that which it fears. It reaches the height of its cherished aspiration; it falls to the level of its unchastened desires, and circumstances are the means by which the soul receives its own."

the Relief Society, MIA, or the priesthood quorum. We can all appreciate the wisdom that information received in interviews be kept confidential. Faith and trust can easily be broken if personal and private matters become "public" business. A leader or one who finds himself in a counseling situation, should always receive approval from the counselee before sharing confidential information with another, even the ecclesiastical authority.

The above would apply in all situations. For example: The head of a house shares a personal problem with his home teacher. Again, the home teacher would not violate confidences but do all in his power to learn the needs of his assigned family and to fulfill them. In the event of a problem that needs the bishop's personal attention, the home teacher becomes the agent or vehicle of building the bridge between the member and his leader. Counseling is terminated only when (1) the individual ceases to want aid or (2) he changes his behavior so he doesn't need help any longer.

Now, let's see how you would handle a problem situation dealing with self-indulgence.

A fellow member of your organization has confided in you that he has a serious problem. He wants to set himself right but doesn't know how to do it. Which of the following represents the best way to direct him?

1. I would determine whether he really wanted to change, counsel with him on how it could be accomplished, and then commit him to an alternative plan that meets his needs more satisfactorily. In subsequent sessions I would try to make certain that he was true to his commitment and plan. (Turn to page 301.)

2. I would explain to him the steps of repentance and tell him what he had to do to overcome his shortcomings. (Turn to page 301.)

"A man does not come to the almshouse or the jail by the tyranny of fate or circumstance, but by the pathway of grovelling thoughts and base desires. Nor does a pure-minded man fall suddenly into crime by stress of any near external force; the criminal thought had long been secretly fostered in the heart, and the hour of opportunity revealed its gathered power. Circumstance does not make the man; it reveals him to himself. No such conditions can exist as descending into vice and its attendant sufferings apart from vicious inclinations, or ascending into virtue and its pure happiness without the continued cultivation of virtuous aspirations; and man, therefore, as the Lord and master of thought, is the maker of himself, the shaper and author of environment. Even at birth, the soul comes to its own and through every step of its earthly pilgrimage it attracts those combinations of conditions which reveal itself which are the reflections of its own purity and impurity, its strength and weakness."

Did you say, "I would determine whether he really wanted to change, counsel with him on how it could be accomplished and then commit him to an alternative plan that meets his needs more satisfactorily"?

You have selected the most difficult alternative, but the one that will be most helpful to him. Usually what a person needs in a situation of this nature is a confidant that will befriend him, express faith in him, show him how he can gain self-control, but never condone his actions.

Did you say, "I would explain to him the steps of repentance and tell him what he had to do to overcome his shortcomings"?

This approach might be extremely helpful if he were able to apply the counsel you give at this time. Unfortunately, knowing what to do, is something quite apart from being able to do it. He also needs someone who will hold him responsible to his committed decision. (Please return to page 299 and select the other alternative.)

2. *Working with problems of pride.*

One of the more common counseling problems a church leader has is dealing with apparent indecisiveness, inadequacy or despair. These are characterized by questions such as: "Should I go to take that new job?" "Should I marry (so and so) even though he is not a member of the Church?" "Should I go on a mission?" The problems are not those of indecisiveness, but what the individual is trying to say is, "I don't have the confidence to make my own decision," or "I don't know how to get an answer to my prayers."

"Men do not attract that which they want, but that which they are."

—James Allen

It is clearly not the counselor's responsibility to make this decision for him, or tell him what he should do in making decisions of this nature. It is the counselor's responsibility to help him discover within himself the resources to make his own decisions.

The counselor may ask him what he has done to weigh all the alternatives in coming to a decision. In many cases, none will have been considered, so he might say, "Let's see if you can't think of one or two right now. I will try to think of some also." At this point, the counselor and the counselee explore all his desires, interests, anxieties, and opinions that have a bearing on the decision. From this conversation should come both a relationship with one another and an understanding of the real problem. The counselor then needs to help the person discover the resources to make his own decision. He does this by giving understanding and assurance that he has the capacity within himself to accomplish his desires. It might be appropriate to refer the individual to his patriarchal blessing as a reinforcement of his abilities and capacities. In the event no blessing has been received, then perhaps encouragement could be given to seek one. Each person needs to make an honest assessment of his capabilities and inadequacies. This may be done by having him write these down outside of the counseling interview. When he returns, these can be discussed and then he can be helped to make a realistic appraisal of himself. But more significantly he needs to know the process of getting answers to prayers. Many of those who come for help expect the Lord to make their decisions. You might read with him from the Doctrine and Covenants, Section 9:7-10, pointing out that he first must make a decision and then bring it to the Lord for confirmation (as discussed in Chapter 1).

Once a person resolves his problem counseling may be terminated by suggesting: "Now that you have found

"Take my yoke upon you, and learn of me; for I am meek and lowly in heart: and ye shall find rest unto your souls."

—Matt. 11:29

THE MALADY:	Mental and physical sin
THE CURE:	Self-mastery
THE VEHICLE:	The Church
THE MEDICATION:	The gospel
THE TREATMENT:	Constructive activity so full of good works there is no time nor thought for evil.

—Spencer W. Kimball

out *how* to solve one problem, you'll be able to solve others that come up the same way, won't you?"

How would you handle this situation?

A student in your class has been dating another member of the Church for some time and they are contemplating marriage. The young lady comes to you and asks, "How do I know that Dale is really the man I should marry?" Which of the following would suggest the best approach to you in helping her solve her problem:

1. Suggest to her that several more months of courtship will resolve most of her concerns. (Turn to page 307.)
2. Talk with her further about the reasons for her insecurity to determine if she really knows herself and then encourage her to pray about it and the Lord will give her an answer. (See below.)

Did you say you would "talk with her further about the reasons for her insecurity and then encourage her to pray about it and the Lord will give her an answer"?

Your choice demonstrates that you understand her uncertainty and indecisiveness as a symptom of a deeper problem. It would be best to explore the basis of her insecurity and then encourage her to seek guidance from the Lord. Prayer is certainly the vital key in making right decisions, but we must be careful not to convey to others that the Lord will make the decision for her. This she must do, and he will confirm her choice if it be correct. (Turn to page 307.)

"A person ceases to be contrary in respect to a desirable conduct only when he himself has had a hand in declaring that course of conduct to be desirable."

—Allport

"A man's word is God in man."

—Tennyson

Did you say you would "suggest to her that she extend her courtship several months and the added time will resolve her uncertainty"?

While longer courtships can do much to resolve problems of uncertainty, time alone is not always the best choice. There may be other reasons for her inability to decide. (Please return to page 305 and select the other alternative.)

3. *Working with problems of self-seeking.*

A problem in this category comes to the attention of church leaders most usually when a fellow worker does not dedicate himself to the assigned responsibility of his job, or he elects to turn down a call of church service. Once an individual has accepted a job and allows worldly aspirations or interests to interfere with the job or his Sundays, it then becomes necessary to counsel with the individual as to which is the priority commitment. A reminder of the commitment made at the time the assignment was given, often is all that is necessary providing he accepts the challenge again. If he elects however, to continue with his outside interests, he needs to know that he has broken his promise and the trust placed in him. This can be said *only if* you have a relationship of trust established. Counseling terminates with problems of this nature when (1) the person decides he no longer wants to be so committed, or (2) the person rededicates his time and talents to his assignment.

In light of the above, what would you counsel in this situation:

A brother who holds a responsible assignment has not paid tithing for the past year, stating that he doesn't earn enough money to pay his tithing and provide a living for his family. He earns an average salary, has a

THE STEPS IN THE COUNSELING PROCESS

1. Establish a relationship of trust and concern for the other person.
2. Get him to talk about his problem.
3. Explore with him the alternatives for a more satisfactory fulfillment.
4. Help him to make a committed plan to achieve his program.
5. Hold him responsible for what he says that he will do, commending him when he takes the course of action that leads to higher need satisfaction.
6. Allow him to become independent of your help.
7. Encourage him to pray.

comfortable home, and spends a good deal of time with his hobby—boating.

1. Release him from his job, but don't explain why. (See below.)

2. Talk to him about his responsibility and commitment to the Lord and give him an opportunity to re-evaluate his goals, purposes and intent. (See below.)

Did you say, "Release him from the job, but don't explain why"?

You may find it necessary to release him from his job, particularly if he elects to put his other interests first. But, he deserves to know the reason why his action is not satisfactory so he can choose between the alternative of dedication, or serving his own interests. (Please see above and select the other alternative.)

Did you say, "Talk to him about his responsibility and commitment to the Lord and give him an opportunity to re-evaluate his goals and intent"?

This would be the better approach since it allows him to choose to rededicate himself to his calling, or serve his own interests, in which case it might then be necessary to suggest the alternative of a release. (Turn to page 311.)

CHAPTER 7 SELF-TEST

1. What is the purpose for counseling in the Church? (Page 263.)
2. How would you describe the most ideal conditions in terms of the following:
   a. the place to hold a counseling interview (Page 265.)
   b. when you should interview another (Page 265.)
   c. the length of a normal counseling interview (Page 267.)
   d. the most desirable seating arrangement. (Page 267.)
3. Indicate what you can do to improve your counseling techniques in the following areas:
   a. establishing a relationship of trust and concern with others (Page 271.)
   b. getting the other person to talk about his problem (Page 281.)
   c. teaching the other person to solve his problems by considering the alternatives that will fulfill his needs with greater satisfaction, and by following through a program with him to see he accomplishes his goals. (Page 291.)

Chapter 8

THE MAN WHO KNOWS HOW TO DELEGATE

At the completion of this chapter, you should be able to:

1. Explain why a leader needs to delegate responsibility and authority.
2. Describe how to determine what authority to delegate.
3. Explain how you can more effectively delegate authority to others.

Chapter 8

THE MAN WHO KNOWS HOW TO DELEGATE

What Does It Mean to Delegate?

Involving everyone creatively in the planning and policy making of an organization builds morale, maintains interest and motivation, and builds good will toward the leader. It is essential to the spirit of an organization.

Defining and delegating responsibility to individuals gets the job done; it makes for efficiency. Committees and groups are good for counsel and mutual stimulation, but it's the individual that gets the job done.

One of the frequent misconceptions in the art of delegating authority is that it is the ability to get someone else to do your job. In conceiving the delegation prerogative to be nothing more than "shifting responsibility," the leader has communicated to the other person, "You will be doing me a great favor if you will complete this task." The co-worker then considers it his prerogative to carry out the task or leave it incomplete. Much of the failure, in any organization, of individuals not doing their assigned jobs can be attributed to this misconception.

The Lord never did intend that one man should have all the power, and for that reason he has placed in His Church, the presidents, apostles, high priests, seventies, elders, and the various officers of the lesser priesthood, all of which are essential in their order and place according to the authority bestowed upon them. The Lord never did anything that was not essential or that was superfluous. There is a use for every branch of the priesthood, and he has established it in his Church. We want every man to learn his duty, and we expect that every man will do his duty as faithfully as he knows how and carry off his portion of the responsibility of building up Zion in the latter days.

—President Joseph F. Smith; quoted by Harold B. Lee, Conf. Rep., April 6, 1963, p. 81

What is Delegation?

To delegate authority is to authorize another person to represent you. He has become entrusted with your power and authority by virtue of the rights you have accorded to him. In short, delegated power is a trust bestowed. It is sharing the prerogatives of your responsibility. On the surface, delegation seems quite simple. All we do is decide what someone else can do to make a job easier and then tell him to do it. But it takes only one experience to discover that the delegating process is more complicated than it appears. Delegating involves the intricate relationships between the most complex and sensitive machines in the world—people.

What happens when one delegates? First, there must be an assignment of duties; second, there must be authority given to perform them; and third, there must be a realization of the responsibility attached. All these must be given or the delegating process has not been complete and will not function effectively.

The "Why" of Delegation

Quite obviously one of the most important reasons for delegating is to increase productivity and make the organization operate more efficiently and effectively. Oftentimes when delegation fails, it is because there has not been adequate preparation. Planning always precedes power.

There are three primary reasons for delegating:

1. *You can't perform the job alone*—Occasionally, we find a leader who feels he is the only person who has sufficient grasp of the job to get it done right. He soon finds himself however, in a state of anxiety and frustra-

And it came to pass . . . that Moses sat to judge the people: and the people stood by Moses from the morning unto the evening. And when Moses' father-in-law saw all that he did to the people, he said, What is this thing that thou doest to the people? Why sittest thou thyself alone, and all the people stand by thee from morning unto even? And Moses said unto his father-in-law, Because the people come unto me to inquire of God: When they have a matter they come unto me; and I judge between one and another, and I do make them know the statutes of God, and his laws. And Moses' father-in-law said unto him. The thing that thou doest is not good. Thou wilt surely wear away, both thou, and this people that is with thee: for this thing is too heavy for thee; THOU ART NOT ABLE TO PERFORM IT THYSELF ALONE. Hearken now unto my voice, I will give thee counsel, and God shall be with thee: Be thou for the people to God-ward, that thou mayest bring the causes unto God: And thou shalt teach them ordinances and laws, and shalt shew them the way wherein they must walk, and the work they must do. Moreover thou shalt provide out of all the people able men, such as fear God, men of truth, hating covetousness; and place such over them, to be rulers of thousands, and rulers of hundreds, rulers of fifties, and rulers of tens: and let them judge the people at all seasons: and it shall be, that every great matter they shall bring unto thee, but every small matter they shall judge: SO SHALL IT BE EASIER FOR THYSELF, and THEY SHALL BEAR THE BURDEN WITH THEE.

Exodus 18:13-22.

tion over the fact that there aren't enough hours in a day to get the job done. About this time, he complains: "How do they expect a man to do all he is supposed to accomplish?" The answer, of course, is to teach others to be effective through delegation.

2. *It will ease your load*—Too frequently capable leaders are burdened down with items of lesser importance in comparison to the major problems that need their attention. For example: It is not uncommon for a bishop to become more concerned about building assessments than the inactive boys in the Aaronic Priesthood program. By giving all of his time to such projects, the more important responsibility—his young people—is left unattended or given secondary consideration. Effective administrators have found that they can lighten their load immensely by giving their attention only to matters that cannot be delegated, and entrusting the responsibility of all other matters to capable co-workers.

3. *Others should bear the burden*—If only the presiding officers of an organization are receiving the blessings of service, the purpose of the program has not been realized. Some leaders feel that they have the capability of doing the job better than another, so they are reluctant to allow others to try. It is hoped that the leader is more capable. But it must be remembered that one of the primary purposes of any organization is to assist *ALL* members in their own spiritual growth and progress. Encouraging others by providing opportunities commensurate with their abilities, even though they may be temporarily inferior, means they will eventually realize their divine capabilities.

Effective Planning

The following is designed to help the leader execute proper delegation:

"Theodore Roosevelt once said that the best executive is the one who has sense enough to pick good men to do what he wants done and self-restraint enough to keep from meddling with them while they do it."

—Sterling W. Sill

1. Establish your objective.
2. Determine the key factors and the alternatives.
3. Get all the facts.
4. Determine the action to be taken.
5. Arrange for the execution of the plan.

Schedule the action. Prepare to delegate responsibility by describing: what, when, where, how, why and who.

React to this statement:

"The art of delegation is the ability to get someone else to do my job more effectively."

1. I would disagree. (See below.)
2. I would agree. (Turn to page 323.)

Did you say, "I would disagree"?

I'm happy you did. Your statement suggests you had in mind that delegated responsibility is a shared responsibility and sharing the assignment, blessings, and difficulties is the most effective means of providing growth opportunity for others. (Turn to page 323.)

What is priesthood? . . . it is the government of God, whether on earth or in the heavens, for it is by that power, agency, or principle that all things are governed on the earth and in the heavens, and by that power that all things are upheld and sustained. It governs all things—it directs all things—it sustains all things—and has to do with all things that God and truth are associated with. It is the power of God delegated to intelligences in the heavens and to men on the earth.

—John Taylor, Millennial Star, Vol. 9:321

Did you say, "I would agree"?

Certainly this is one way of looking at delegating responsibility. There is an objection to this definition however, and that is: it conveys to another that the leader is merely shifting his responsibility. Too often this approach gives the person the idea that he is doing the leader a personal favor if he undertakes the job. (Please return to page 321 and consider the other alternative.)

Priesthood Authority

Priesthood is the power and authority of God delegated to man on earth to act in all things for the salvation of men. Thus priesthood holders share the power of the Lord; they receive a delegation of power and authority from him and are authorized to act in his place and stead in furthering his plans and purposes.

Keys are the right of presidency, the right and power to direct the manner in which others use their priesthood. In their fulness they are held by but one man at a time on earth, the President of the Church. He confers keys upon others, thus empowering them to work in assigned positions of presidency and to direct the labors of designated priesthood holders. Through this system perfect control is maintained, and all of the Lord's agents, acting pursuant to the specific delegation of authority received, carry on "our Father's business." In this way each priesthood holder, using delegated authority, is able to act in the field of his assignment in carrying on the work of the Church.

A leader does not lose his authority nor his responsibility when he delegates it. He must still remain primarily responsible. And he must guarantee the success of the one to whom the responsibility is delegated. He cannot delegate and then turn his back on what occurs afterward. He must inspect; he must train; he must encourage; he must supervise the one to whom the responsibility has been given. No one can delegate away his responsibility. He delegates his responsibility without losing it. Delegation without control is irresponsibility. Nor has there been any real delegation if the responsibility has not been fully accepted. Incompetence or unwillingness of an individual to accept responsibility should not go undiscovered or uncorrected. Rather, such unwillingness should be immediately known to the one who still holds the primary responsibility.

But just as delegation is not abdiction, neither does the acceptance of responsibility mean usurpation. Each must work within the limits of church policy and the authority given to him. He must also work under the direction of him to whom he is responsible. . . . He must know the individual to whom he is giving authority and be sure that the assignment comes within the individual's capacity and that he can and will devote the time to carry out the assignment properly.

—Sterling W. Sill, *Leadership,* Volume I
(Salt Lake City: Bookcraft, 1958), p. 213.

Authority Which Can and Cannot Be Delegated

Some authority of the priesthood cannot be delegated to another, but must remain with the individual holding the specific keys. For example: A bishop may give the authority to another priesthood bearer to be an adviser to a priests quorum, but he cannot delegate the responsibility to any other priesthood holder to preside over the quorum. As president to the priests quorum, he alone holds the keys of presiding until released.

Another case in point is the stake president's assignment as the presiding officer over the high priests quorum. He may not delegate this presiding authority to any one else within the stake.

No presiding officer can delegate his presiding authority to another individual, though he may delegate the authority to conduct meetings, or to officiate in the priesthood or to accomplish a specified assignment.

Leaders need to keep uppermost in mind that when responsibility is given, authority to act should go with the assignment. Nothing is more discouraging to an individual, to whom responsibility has been given, than to have no authority to act. He is thus a "puppet" in the organization. At the time a job is assigned, a clear definition of its responsibilities should be outlined and the authority to act given.

The person to whom authority is delegated, should also understand the limitations of his assignment in terms of what prerogatives belong to presiding officials over him.

"A good leader takes the position that the other fellow is capable of being far more than he is, and it is the leader's responsibility to help him develop to his fullest potential."

—Lawrence A. Appley

"Real leaders are strong individuals but are never soloists. They solicit help and capitalize on the strength of the people they lead."

—Adam S. Bennion

Test your understanding of proper delegation of authority by responding to the statements below. Indicate with a circle whether the statement is true or false.

1. T F When a leader confers authority upon another, he is absolved from further responsibility.
2. T F A bishop should delegate all his authority to his counselors.
3. T F Presiding authority cannot be delegated.
4. T F The priesthood is God's power delegated to man.

(Turn to page 329 for answers.)

Effective Delegation

Once a person has been called to an assignment, it is the obligation of a leader to make certain he understands all of the duties in connection with it. The same conditions of dignity and privacy of conversation that are important to the calling interview (see Chapter 4), also apply to the interview wherein the assignment is outlined and the delegation of authority given. Ample time should be allowed for a discussion of problems and any questions. The following are suggestions which will aid in conducting a successful "delegation of authority and responsibility" interview.

1. *A person needs to understand his specific area of responsibility*—In most cases the leader can accomplish this by thoroughly reviewing instructional manuals pertaining to the person's calling.

2. *A person needs to understand where he fits into the over-all program*—This may often be done by the

Samson was a beautiful dapple-gray horse with a splendid physique and such height that he seemed to tower above all the other horses. But, though large, he was gentle and friendly and everyone was attracted to him.

Samson was a chain horse and stood daily at the foot of a steep hill waiting for the heavy loads that had to be pulled. Samson always pulled in front of the other horses. When the lorry with the load would come, he would prick up his ears and stamp his feet eagerly—it meant an opportunity to show his strength.

Samson was an exhibitionist. When his keeper led him to the load and attached his chains to the shaft, he did not wait for the other horses—he was a Samson. Head down, knees almost touching the ground, sparks flying from his hooves, he practically pulled the whole weight by himself. He would not allow the other horses to pull their share.

Samson's keeper was asked why Samson was not given a rest from his chain horse position, and put into the shafts like the other horses. He replied that Samson wouldn't pull when back with the others; he couldn't show off there.

He didn't seem to be able to cooperate; he had to be out in front doing everything by himself.

One day Samson wasn't standing at the bottom of the hill, but another horse was in his place. Samson was dead. He had died of overwork. He had pulled too hard alone.

Many leaders are like Samson, wanting all the work and glory for themselves and refusing to cooperate with others. The power of any good organization is a combined power, and it is wasted by those who try to pull the whole load alone.

Wise leaders share responsibility.

leader before the total group of personnel in his organization. However, it is helpful in the private interview—when specific details of the job assignment are discussed—to show briefly how this person's job relates to the total organization. In other words, the person must be made to feel that he is part of a "team effort."

3. *A person needs to understand the criteria for effectiveness*—"How do I know when I'm doing an effective job?" is a pertinent question to organizational leaders. The individual needs to understand clearly how you, the leader, are going to measure his effectiveness so he knows where he stands. This might be done by giving him a brief explanation of the follow-up system of your organization. For example: You might say, "You are probably wondering how we determine the effectiveness of our teachers. Each month we hold a meeting in which we discuss each member under your care. At this time we expect that you will give us a well-thought-out report on the status of each student's activity, what you are presently doing to help each one, and what we can do to help you in your efforts. This report should be in writing so it can be reviewed by us and the bishop."

Following are the correct answers to the test previously given:

1. False Whenever a leader confers authority upon another, his job has just begun. He now has to effectively follow-up on the delegated responsibility to see that it has been carried out to his expectations.
2. False A bishop cannot delegate his presiding authority to his counselors or to anyone else.
3. True
4. True

A leader is best
When people barely know that he exists,
Not so good when people follow and acclaim him,
Worse when they obey and despise him,
"Fail to honor people,
  They fail to honor you."
But of a good leader, who talks little,
When his work is done, his aim fulfilled,
They will all say, "We did this ourselves."

—Loatzu

4. *A person needs to know what responsibility and authority he has*—At this point the leader will want to define the limitations of the person's responsibility. For example: The individual should know how his duties relate to that of another in the same organization, and to the various leaders under whom he labors.

5. *A person needs to know the "chain of command."* —Workers in the Church learn a real lesson from the military. One of the first things a new recruit learns is the "chain of command," or the established line of communication and authority. If a recruit wants to discuss

a matter with his senior officer, he must begin his journey through the chain of command, namely the person directly over him.

As individuals come to learn the line of authority in their organization the burden upon all is immediately reduced.

Frequently a presiding officer will receive complaints and requests for assistance from an individual that has bypassed other leaders within the organization. It is important that the leader in such a situation point out to the individual the need to work with the officer over him.

6. *A person needs to know that his leaders have confidence in his ability*—This is best demonstrated by

Remember your co-workers will produce more and will be happier if they know:

1. what they are supposed to do
2. what authority they have
3. what their relationships are with regard to other people
4. what constitutes a job well done in terms of specific results.

(1) withdrawing completely from the delegated area given to him and let him perform his assigned duty; (2) sustain him, whenever possible, in his actions before others; and (3) express appreciation to him for what he is doing.

Respond to the following situation:

> Just as Bishop Harris was finishing his evening meal, Sister Bradshaw phoned to ask permission to see him. She said it was urgent, and her voice indicated that she was terribly upset. Even though he had a meeting to attend, he arranged to meet her in his office within the hour. Upon meeting, Sister Bradshaw burst into tears, and said, "I just can't stand to teach that class another time. Those children are simply incorrigible; such rudeness you wouldn't find among heathen children. I think you had better find a replacement for me and soon."

When authority has been delegated which of the following alternatives demonstrate the best way to handle this situation?

1. The bishop should refer her to the organizational presidency under whose direction she is teaching. (See below.)
2. The bishop should counsel her in handling the problem situation herself. (Turn to page 335.)

Did you say, "The bishop should refer her to the organizational presidency under whose direction she is teaching"?

You are right! This is what happened in this situation.

After trying to console her and finding out the exact details of her discipline problem, the bishop wisely asked, "Have you discussed this with Sister Callister or Sister Johnson?" (Sister Johnson was the president of the organization and Sister Callister was her counselor, whose assignment was supervision of the age group taught by Sister Bradshaw.) To which she replied, "No bishop, I knew you'd be able to help."

Then Bishop Harris kindly explained the order of authority to Sister Bradshaw, and wisely referred her to Sister Callister. It would have been easy for him to have helped her solve the problem, but in so doing, he would have released at least three people: Sister Callister, Sister Johnson, and Brother Anderson who was his counselor assigned to the particular organization. (Turn to page 337.)

Did you say, "The bishop should counsel her in handling the problem situation herself"?

Oops! You just released the presidency of the organization in which she is a teacher. If the bishop assumes the authority he delegated to them, it is comparable to effecting their release for he has refused to acknowledge their authority and responsibility. This is one of the hardest of all lessons to learn because of our desire to be helpful, but for the sake of the organizational leaders who may serve under you, it is a vital consideration to remember. (Please return to page 333 and select the other alternative.)

CHAPTER 8 SELF-TEST

1. State briefly in your words why a leader in the Church today should delegate authority to others. (Page 317.)
2. How can a leader determine what authority should be delegated and what should be retained? (Page 325.)
3. What can you do—starting immediately—to more effectively delegate authority to others? (Page 327.)

Chapter 9

THE MAN WHO KNOWS HOW TO FOLLOW THROUGH

At the completion of this chapter you should be able to:

1. EXPLAIN THE NEED FOR PROPER FOLLOW-THROUGH PROCEDURE.
2. DESCRIBE THE STEPS A LEADER SHOULD TAKE TO ENSURE SUCCESSFUL FOLLOW-THROUGH PROCEDURE.
3. STATE WHAT YOU INTEND TO DO IN YOUR ASSIGNMENT TO ENSURE MORE EFFECTIVE FOLLOW-THROUGH METHODS.

Chapter 9

THE MAN WHO KNOWS HOW TO FOLLOW THROUGH

The Importance of Follow-through

It is not enough to define and delegate responsibilities among officers and members of an organization. Once authority has been delegated and the individual trained in his task, it is most essential that a leader have a genuine follow-through system by which he measures the success in the assignment given.

In professional baseball one of the most important and difficult lessons a pitcher must learn is the skill of following through with the pitching motion after the ball is released. This is the process of throwing a ball toward a target—home plate—and then instead of stopping the motion of the arm, it is allowed to go around in front of the body and to the opposite side. The purpose of the follow-through in any sport, be it golf, tennis, boxing, baseball, football, basketball, or soccer is to ensure accuracy, maximum power behind the throwing or kicking effort, and continuous motion so one does not strain the muscles of the arm.

Certain attitudes and procedures are essential to the successful operation of this principle of leadership. Here are two:

1. The head of an organization should respect each

"Good leadership consists of showing average people how to do the work of superior people."

—John D. Rockefeller

member and officer in the organization. How can this be done? First, by reviewing the responsibilities of each officer from time to time; second, by providing opportunities for them to use their initiative; third, by calling for reports regularly; and fourth, by giving credit and appreciation, both privately and publicly, for work well done.

2. Each individual's plans should be checked before execution begins. There are a number of reasons for such action. It ensures that:

a. the job will be performed to the expectations of his training and minimum standard.

b. the assignment will be performed on schedule.

c. the persons performing will be able to adapt to changing circumstances by keeping continuously appraised of the facts.

d. the person responsible for the assignment will be able to achieve some of the immediate targets toward accomplishing the whole of the objective.

"A good leader inspires other men with confidence in *him:* A great leader inspires them with confidence in themselves.

Which of the following best expresses the major reason for effective follow-through?

1. It lets the other person know that you are a "take-charge" individual and will see a job through to completion. (See below.)

2. It ensures that an assignment will be completed on time and according to the understood expectations. (See below.)

Did you say, "It lets the other person know that you are a "take-charge" individual and will see a job through to completion"?

This may be one of the effects of follow-through, but it is not the primary reason. The main purpose is to let fellow workers know what is expected of them, the method of accounting for progress, and the time allotted to complete the assignment. (Please check above and select the other alternative.)

Did you say, "It ensures that an assignment will be completed on time and according to the understood expectations"?

This is the major reason for an effective follow-through system. This answer suggests that the leader does three things:

1. He makes certain that people understand their job requirements.

2. He has them report on their progress, and

3. He makes certain they understand when they are to report.

Let's discuss these in detail. (Please turn to page 347.)

JESUS TEACHES, DELEGATES, FOLLOWS THROUGH

1. He taught and trained apostles in their duties by demonstration. (Taught and trained.)

2. He ordained them in the priesthood and conferred upon them the keys of the kingdom to administer the affairs of the kingdom. (Delegated authority.)

3. He sent them out to heal, preach and teach and requested that they report back to him telling of their successes. (Follow through.)

Successful Follow-through Procedures

There are certain essential steps that need to be taken if a leader is to ensure successful follow-through on delegated assignments. In other words, the person to whom authority and responsibility has been given needs to understand the basis on which his success will be measured. Following are several important considerations:

1. *A person needs to understand the minimum standard required*—This means that time should be taken to explain the assignment, relationships, and expectations of a minimum stand of performance. For example: If a new teacher trainer has just been called, some of the duties and expectations which might be stressed are:

a. diligent preparation of lesson materials

b. attendance at ward council meetings as requested

c. attendance at a monthly faculty meeting and stake preparation meeting

d. attendance at a weekly prayer meeting

e. living a life that reflects the message one teaches.

Once the individual understands his obligations and commits himself to them, he will feel that all the responsibilities attendant to the assignment are vital.

2. *A person needs to understand how to report assignments*—As will be demonstrated, there are several effective ways in which one may report the progress of his assignment. More important than the method of follow-through is a clear understanding of *how* the leader expects the individual to report to him. For example: A bishop may desire to have an oral and a

"The power to lead is the power to mislead; and the power to mislead is the power to destroy."

—Elder Thomas S. Monson

written report presented to the ward council once a month on the activity status of each young person in an auxiliary organization. If that is the desire, then this must be explained to the individual who is responsible for such reporting. If he desires that the report be uniformly given by all executives, then this process of reporting needs to be explained.

3. *The person needs to understand the date the report is expected*—Whenever there is a definite date or time in which a scheduled project has to be completed, this needs to be clearly communicated to all who are responsible for it. This is especially true where a written or oral report is due by a designated date. Successful leaders have found that it is best to tell the person, at the time of his call, that reports must be submitted promptly and if they are not, he can expect to be contacted, either by phone or a personal visit.

Regardless of the method it is imperative that the leader do what he said he would. If, for example, a report is expected the leader will need to hold the person accountable for it every time. Unless this is done, the importance of the procedure will be minimized to all involved.

Which statement best describes the steps a leader should take to ensure successful follow-through on a delegated assignment?

1. The leader should allow the person to do the job to the best of his ability, providing follow-through only when the individual does not do his assignment. (Turn to page 351.)

2. The leader should give the person a clear understanding of what is to be minimally expected and then describe the time and method of follow-through. (Turn to page 351.)

WHAT IS PAR?

It is . . . .

P -lanning

A -ction

R -eporting

Did you say, "The leader should allow the person to do the job to the best of his ability providing follow-through only when the individual does not do his assignment"?

By selecting this alternative, you have indicated that instead of the follow-through procedure being used as a method to ensure success it is only a method of correction. Of course, it is much more than this.

Corrections will need to be made, but these should be made during the training period. The follow-through procedure is a continuous process of determining, at a given time, the progress and status of the delegated task. (Please return to page 349 and select the other alternative.)

Did you say, "The leader should give the person a clear understanding of what is to be minimally expected of him, then describe the time and method of follow-through"?

Exactly. Anything short of this sets the stage for failure in the assignment.

Effective Methods in Following Through

Some follow-through methods which have been found successful by leaders are:

1. *Written reports*—One of the most common types of reporting procedures used is the written report which gives a statistical summary of a particular activity.

Nothing is ever done beautifully which is done in rivalship, nor nobly which is done in pride.

—Ruskin

Some leaders use a variation of this reporting procedure by having their workers submit to them a monthly summary of the activity status of each person in the organization. Such follow-through procedures help the leaders see at a glance those who are in need of attention.

Another variation of the written report is to have all of those in the program summarize their suggestions and/or plans so that their ideas can be studied and considered by all. An example of this variation would be where a ward or branch was faced by a unique situation not covered by the handbook, so that adaptive procedures may need to be taken. Such a situation exists in some areas of the Church where the full church program cannot always be offered.

2. *Checklists*—An effective follow-through procedure for any function or activity is the checklist. A checklist is illustrated on page 193. The advantage of using this device is that it sets down all the things necessary to ensure success. It also designates who is responsible for the assignment, and the date it is to be completed. It has the advantage of relieving the frustration of last minute details since, by following the checklist, these will have already been taken care of.

3. *Oral evaluations*—A recent development within church priesthood leadership is the oral evaluation. This involves the home teacher reporting to his priesthood leader who in turn reports to the bishop. All communication and follow-through in the priesthood should theoretically go through this pipeline of authority.

In addition to giving a written report to a leader, the home teacher discusses "orally, in depth, the status of his 'charges' and considers many items beyond those which could be written satisfactorily."

Suggest rather than command or demand.

Give credit without failure to the proper persons and sources.

The oral interview has many other applications outside of home teaching. It may be used as a follow-through procedure on projects, reports, or any type of activity or proposal.

Among the questions that might be asked by leaders of the person to whom responsibility has been delegated are the following:

a. Were the plans mutually agreed upon, followed?

b. What problems did you encounter in accomplishing the assignment?

c. What did you do to solve these problems?

d. Is there a better method you would recommend on the basis of your experience with this assignment?

e. What can we do to help you?

4. *Report meetings*—The report meeting has been found to be a helpful method in determining the problems of individuals affected by an organization or in determining their spiritual attitude. Many leaders have found it helpful to have the oral report supplemented by a written report. Others have learned that those in the organization will express their testimony and attitude toward the work in their reports when asked: "As you give your reports today would you briefly tell us how you feel about your assignment and make any recommendations you feel would be helpful."

The report meeting can be used in any organization of the Church. To ensure a beneficial outcome of such a meeting the following need to be considered:

a. Each individual needs to understand the specific areas of responsibility for which he is accountable.

Preserve an open mind on all debatable questions. Discuss, but don't argue. It is a mark of superior minds to disagree and yet be friendly. "However, some open minds should be closed for repairs."

b. Each individual should understand that he is responsible for giving a report on his delegated responsibility.

c. Each individual should understand that the purpose of the report is to accurately assess the total organization, suggest ways for improvement, and make recommendations in accordance with his observations and feelings.

Remember, no one will report what ought to be reported until the "climate of trust" has been created and a "feeling of trust" established.

How would you handle the following situation in terms of applying follow-through methods?

A new athletic director has just been called to serve in your branch. A number of important athletic events are to be scheduled in the district during the next four months for the purpose of involving young people of all ages. The new athletic director has a great deal of enthusiasm for his assignment, but very little experience. How would you help to ensure his success?

1. I would give him supervised instruction with at least one major athletic event, demonstrating how to do the job, and then follow-through thereafter by getting him to report on his progress at report meetings. (See below.)

2. I would allow him to function in his job for a short time giving him proper encouragement since he doesn't have much experience, and offer to help him if he feels it is necessary. (Turn to page 359.)

Did you say, "I would give him supervised instruction with at least one major athletic event, demonstrating how to do the job, and then follow-through thereafter by getting him to report on his progress at report meetings"?

This is excellent! Such procedure will demonstrate to him that you are really sincere in helping him be effective in his job. (Turn to page 361.)

Did you say, "I would allow him to function in his job for a short time giving him proper encouragement since he doesn't have much experience, and then offer to help him if he feels it is necessary"?

Giving him the encouragement he will need is excellent but, you are letting him determine what the standard of performance will be in relation to his assignment. If you wait for him to request help, it may be too late. It is better to train the individual to the standard of performance first, rather than to have to change his standard to reach the minimum requirements for an effective job. (Turn to page 357 and select the other alternative.)

CHAPTER 9 SELF-TEST

1. If you were asked to justify the need for a proper follow-through system in your ogranization, what would you answer? (Page 341.)
2. Three steps were cited as being important to successful follow-through procedures. In what way are they helpful to you? (Page 347.)
3. On a sheet of paper, state briefly what you can do in your present assignment to accomplish more effective follow-through procedure by utilizing one or several of the suggested methods in this chapter. (Page 351.)

Chapter 10

THE MAN WHO IS AWARE

At the completion of this chapter you should be able to:

1. SEE MORE VIVIDLY THE NEED TO BE PROMPT, FAIR, AND FACTUAL IN ALL OF YOUR DEALINGS.

2. ACHIEVE GREATER SELF-CONFIDENCE BY LEARNING WAYS AND MEANS OF OVERCOMING PERSONAL LIMITATIONS BY USING SELF-CONTROL.

3. PERFORM YOUR ASSIGNMENT WITH GREATER INTEREST AND ENTHUSIASM.

Chapter 10

THE MAN WHO IS AWARE

One of Ripley's famous cartoons pictured a plain bar of iron worth $5.00. This same bar of iron when made into horseshoes would be worth $10.50. If made into needles, it would be worth $3,285.00, and if turned into balance springs for watches, its worth becomes $250,000.00. The same is true of another kind of material—YOU! Believe it or not!

The previous nine chapters have dealt with the basic ingredients and attributes which are essential in building successful leaders and in refining people. But important as they are, a leader cannot be totally effective until he becomes aware of the following five areas and includes them in his way of life.

1. *Be prompt*—Have you ever thought of the inconsistency of our modern way of life—that everyone is always in a hurry, yet few people ever get any place on time, except of course, to meet certain compulsory appointments. Has it occurred to you also that this very fact offers a wide-open opportunity for one who is prompt to gain a favorable position in the eyes of his fellowmen?

If we were living in a place where railroad trains stopped along the way for conductors to hunt rabbits, if we had no inter-urban cars to catch, no meetings to attend, no banquets or theatres or parties to attend, if we were not pulled by a multitude of demands that

"Well arranged time is the mark of a well arranged mind."

"The only people who can save time are those who spend it well."

make swift action so necessary, perhaps it wouldn't matter. But in the midst of such a swiftly moving society the one who receives our recognition and gains our good favor is the one who, by his promptness and dependability, makes it easy for us to keep in motion.

I remember reading of an old man who said that he had lived to be ninety years of age, and during that time had spent thirty years waiting for other people. I suspect that most of us, not nearly so aged, feel like saying much the same thing. True, we joke about it and laugh at the people who always come late. But the fact remains that beneath this smile is a deep respect for the man or woman who, when he promises to be present at a 7 o'clock meeting, will be present at 7 o'clock and not a moment later.

"I expect to pass through this world but once. Any good therefore that I can do, or any kindness that I can show to any fellow creature, let me do it now. Let me not defer or neglect it, for I shall not pass this way again."

—Stephen Grellet

But there is another and more important reason for being on time. Horace Mann, one of our early educators, said: "Unfaithfulness in the keeping of an appointment is an act of clear dishonesty. You may as well borrow a person's money as his time." And when you borrow his time you are taking, as Benjamin Franklin would say, the most precious of all possessions, something which when lost can never be found, when taken away can never be returned.

I see a Sunday School teacher in his classroom with thirty students before him. The class has commenced, the roll taken, and teacher and students have reached a point of definite interest in their discussion, when the door opens and in walks a tardy student. The eyes of all the class are turned in his direction, the teacher pauses in his discussion, and for a period of at least 60 seconds the work, or at least the attention, of the group is suspended. One minute for each of thirty students, and one teacher, or a total of more than half an hour of valuable time was wasted for the class as a whole by the tardiness of one person. And we have all seen the time when classroom discussions or church meetings have been practically ruined by the straggling in of tardy people at the wrong moment.

What shall we say of these people, as well as those who are called and appointed to direct meetings and programs who carelessly keep others waiting. They actually rob people of their valuable time. Are they criminals? No, we can hardly call them that. Thieves? Perhaps that also is too strong a term for people who do not realize the inconvenience and waste that they are causing. But certainly we are justified in asking such people to read and reread and say to themselves with Horace Mann: "Unfaithfulness in keeping an appointment (or being late) is an act of clear dishonesty. You may as well borrow a person's money as his time," and again with Benjamin Franklin: "If time be all

"Time waits for no one."

things most precious, wasting time must be the greatest prodigality, since lost time is never found again."

If we summon all of the leading business and professional men and women of the world and ask them to speak to those interested in achieving something worthwhile in any field of endeavor, they would include among the first principles to commit and follow: "Be prompt in the keeping of appointments; be prompt in calling and conducting of meetings and whenever possible be prompt in the accomplishment of any task that is committed to your hand." Remember much is gained each day that we do not waste a moment of another's time. It may be more precious to him than silver or gold.

2. *Be fair—get the facts*—It seems almost outmoded in today's world to suggest that people be fair but I venture to say that the majority of tragedies involving human relations could easily be averted if people before attempting to form any judgment were to have all the facts in hand.

Be fair—get the facts.

"Self-confidence is the first requirement to great undertakings."

"The greatest mistake you can make in life is to be continually fearing you will make one."

If only we could be as fair as President Herbert Hoover when, learning of his defeat, said: "I have lost, but I shall be as loyal to those who have defeated me as I should have wished them to be to me if I had won." As fair with truth as the teacher, who, after spending years in the writing of a book on science and discovering one little fact that disproved his theory, withdrew his book and began the task of rewriting; fair as the Savior who, although misunderstood and mistreated by the ones whom he attempted to help, continued to love them and to help them and finally die for them, because, as he said, they knew not what they did.

Now I know that it is exceedingly difficult to be so fair. But I am convinced that it is possible, if one will remember and practice a simple rule: Before doing or saying anything that may cause sorrow or misunderstanding, be sure you know the facts.

I think often of two grocery executives who had a misunderstanding. The feeling grew into hatred, business relations were stopped and the two would not speak to each other. After several years the difficulty was discovered. One man had said something about the other which was perfectly harmless. The words were quoted by a third party just as they were spoken. It was a difference in the tone of voice that had changed a harmless statement into one of poison.

But it is not enough to know the facts. One day while I was riding with some friends in a country I was viewing for the first time, we were having quite a discussion about the beauty of the countryside. "How beautiful!" said one of the travelers.

"I can't see anything beautiful about it," I said. "It is rather dull and so unsightly."

"Why," said my associates, "you're certainly mistaken. It's a most attractive and inspiring scene."

"Master yourself and you can master anything."

—Proverb

"Men were born to succeed, not to fail."

—Henry David Thoreau

"I can't see it that way," I said. And then as I raised my hand to my face to wipe away the perspiration I discovered, what I had entirely forgotten, that I was wearing a pair of dark sunglasses. Pulling them off I realized then that I had been wrong. The scenery was truly bright and beautiful. The sunglasses had played the trick.

And so it is that dark emotions, such as anger and suspicion and fear and self-pride, may come between our minds and very normal situations, making fools of our judgment and causing us, with all of the facts directly in front of us, to arrive at conclusions that are entirely unfair to the situation at hand.

3. *Use self-control*—All of the talent in the world cannot help a leader who fails to discipline himself. I remember seeing a very funny thing a number of years ago while attending the university. A very capable educator had good naturedly sworn that he would not commit another sin as long as he lived. He said he had made a lot of mistakes in the past but from that time on he was going to exercise perfect self-control. And when someone joked him about his resolution he became so angry that he wanted to fight.

Be calm.

"You may not be what you think you are but what you think, you are."

"There is far more opportunity than there is ability."

—Thomas A. Edison

He would never make another mistake. Well, I guess the poor fellow didn't realize that the ability to control one's self in the time of temptation is one that can be developed only after much painstaking practice and sometimes one has to work all kinds of tricks on himself to hold his emotions in leash. But an energetic person works hard and studies several hours a day sometimes to develop other types of ability. Why is it not worth some practice to gain control over one's emotions? I believe that it is, but I am quite sure, from my own experience, that it is no easy job. Suppose we look at some of the plans that others have found helpful.

When Charles Lindbergh was asked what method he used, he said that he came to the conclusion that if he knew the difference between the right way to do a thing and the wrong way to do it, it was up to him to train himself to do the right thing at all times. So he drew up a list of characteristics that he wished to develop and wrote them, one under the other, on the left side of a sheet of paper. Then each evening he would read off the entire list of characteristics. After those that he felt he had developed to some extent during the day he would place a red cross, and after those character factors that he felt he had violated during the day he would draw a black cross. Those he had not been called upon to demonstrate that day would receive no mark. After checking himself in this way over a definite period of time, he would compare the number of red and black crosses and see whether he was getting better or worse. He said that he was generally glad to note improvement as he grew older. He had altogether 58 character factors, among which were: altruism, calmness in temper, clean speech, justice, modesty, no sarcasm, punctuality, etc.

EQUIPMENT

Figure it our for yourself, my lad,
You've all *that* the greatest of men have had,
Two arms, two hands, two legs, two eyes
And brain to use if you would be wise.
With this equipment they all began,
So start for the top and say, "I can."

Look them over, the wise and great,
They take their food from a common plate,
And similar knives and forks they use,
With similar laces they tie their shoes,
The world considers them brave and smart,
But you've all they had when they made their start.

You can triumph and come to skill
You can be great if you only will.
You're well equipped for what fight you choose,
You have legs and arms and a brain to use,
And the man who has risen great deeds to do
Began his life with no more than you.

You are the handicap you must face,
You are the one who must choose your place,
You must say where you want to go,
How much you will study the truth to know.
God has equipped you for life, but He
Lets you decide what you want to be.

Courage must come from the soul within,
The man must furnish the will to win.
So figure it out for yourself, my lad.
You were born with all that the great have had,
With your equipment they all began
Get hold of yourself, and say: *"I can."*

—Edgar A. Guest

Another method that one of our leaders has used successfully is to write each desirable characteristic on a separate card so classifying them that there will be as many cards as there are days in the month. We'll say that on one card is written the word "sincerity." Today that card will be looked at the first thing in the morning and placed in his pocket. Although the person tries every day to be sincere, on this day he will take particular pains to keep this characteristic in mind and to practice it. Tomorrow another card is used, and so on until the month has passed, and each of the wholesome characteristics has held for one day a special place in the thinking and acting of the owner. The plan is carried out in following months with the same group of cards. Now, I suspect that such a scheme would not work advantageously with all, but the leader who advocates it declares that he has found it to be very helpful to many.

Others have noticed considerable development in character by picking a person, who has achieved an extraordinary degree of moral strength, and then judging all actions of life by the life of this ideal. Have I been as kind in all my dealings this day as he would have been? If not, then I need to be more careful tomorrow. Do I have as perfect control of my temper? Am I as sympathetic? Do I go out of my way as much as he, to help the one in trouble? Only when we can say "yes" to such questions dealing with the whole field of moral endeavor, may we be satisfied with our accomplishment of self-control. If we pick some personality that is sufficiently perfect, we shall, no doubt, be struggling upward to the end of our lives.

Many church leaders testify to the value of picking Jesus Christ as an ideal and trying in every activity of the day to do as he would do if he were in the same situation today. Reaching back as it does over a period of nearly, 2,000 years, to a time when conditions were

"A smile is a light in the window of the soul indicating that the heart is at home."

"A little smile adds a great deal to your face value."

"Most folks are about as happy as they make up their minds to be."

—Abraham Lincoln

"Wrinkles should merely indicate where smiles have been."

—Mark Twain

"Nothing great was ever achieved without enthusiasm."

—Ralph Waldo Emerson

quite different from those of the present day, one senses the difficulty of knowing in every case what Jesus would do. Yet in the face of this obstacle, I have a feeling that our very attempt to catch his spirit and follow his example—the example of the greatest personality of all time—will prove a constant stimulus to higher living in the present day.

4. *Be enthusiastic*—Must you be "born" enthusiastic in order to practice and enjoy enthusiasm? Absolutely not! One of the most successful men I've ever known was asked, "How do you always manage to act so bright and enthusiastic? It must be a natural gift. You must have been born with a great supply of enthusiasm." "Not at all," the dynamic leader replied. "I have no greater natural supply of enthusiasm than anyone else. It's just that I USE MINE!"

Whether you realize it or not, you're actually loaded with enthusiasm, which you can utilize readily and almost automatically for tremendous personal benefits. All you have to do is use your enthusiasm every hour of every day, so that it becomes a natural part of you—like breathing. Let's look at some of the simple rules to follow.

The following three lines may well be among the most important you'll ever read. You must do more than just read them. You must learn them, commit them to memory, make them part of your philosophy of living:

If you'll look enthusiastic . . .

And act enthusiastic . . .

You will be enthusiastic!

It never fails; in essence, if you'll do the things that enthusiastic people do—you'll discover that you are enthusiastic. There's no question about it. Read those three lines over again—fix them in your consciousness.

A SMILE

A smile costs nothing, but gives much. It enriches those who receive, without making poorer those who give. It takes but a moment, but the memory of it sometimes lasts forever. None is so rich or mighty that he can get along without it, and none is so poor but that he can be made rich by it. A smile creates happiness in the home, fosters good will in business, and is the countersign of friendship. It brings rest to the weary, cheer to the discouraged, sunshine to the sad, and it is nature's best antidote for trouble. Yet it cannot be bought, begged, borrowed, or stolen, for it is something that is of no value to anyone until it is given away. Some people are too tired to give you a smile. Give them one of yours, as none needs a smile so much as he who has no more to give.

—Author Unknown

How to Look Enthusiastic

The act of smiling is certainly not new and yet note the difference it makes in your appearance. A smile

Be enthusiastic.

says, "I am glad to see you" and is more likely to get an automatic response from the other fellow that he's glad to see you too. The easiest and surest way for you to have people smile at you is for you to smile at them. Practice smiling when you get up in the morning—when you are applying face powder—when you are looking in the mirror and shaving. Every time you wash up during the day, look at the reflection of your face and SMILE. Even at bedtime, as you brush your teeth, look in the mirror and smile. Let's try another: Put aside this book for a minute and walk across the room and back again in the way you usually do. Now, answer this question: Did you hold your head high, or low? Check yourself again. This time note particularly how you held your head, then remember—the enthusiastic person always holds his head high.

"Behold the turtle: He makes progress only when he sticks his neck out."

—James Bryant Conant

"Lift where you stand."

—Edward Everett

"Man is effective in the world not only through what he does, but above all through what he is."

—Rudolph Steiner

"Even on the right track, you'll be run over if you just sit there."

"Opposition only makes the enthusiast more determined."

How to Act Enthusiastic

The great industrialist, Charles Schwab, was noted especially as an executive who secured amazing cooperation from the people who worked about him and those with whom he had business relations. When he was asked what he considered the prime ingredient that had helped make him such a towering success, he answered: "I consider my ability to arouse enthusiasm among people the greatest asset I possess." His ability to arouse enthusiasm among others was due greatly to the fact that, as a big part of his optimistic approval to things, he was always lavish in his praise of the work done by others. In every possible way, he acted to avoid condemning or downgrading others.

This great leader believed firmly in the terse statement made by another very successful man: "Any fool can condemn and downgrade others—and most fools do!"

Taking the positive position, you can profit from the advice of the philosopher, William James, who asserted so wisely, "One of the deepest drives of people is to be appreciated." Ask yourself—have I this practice and habit of the enthusiastic leader, to appreciate the good that others do, and to show my appreciation? When working with others remember that there are two ways to act. Remind yourself to act to lift the other fellow up, not to push him down.

5. *Be optimistic*—Several years ago while serving in the armed forces in the South Pacific, my infantry division was located for a short while on a tiny island where the natives had some very unusual customs. One of the most interesting was the tradition where all its inhabitants were supposed to wear a string of large, green beads, to the end of which was fastened three tiny shells, an ornament intended for the purpose of

Batter up! The batter stands at the plate with the ball speeding toward him at the rate of a hundred and fifty miles per hour. In a third of a second he must size up the throw and decide what to do about it.

No wonder batters in baseball fail to hit more often than they succeed. Even the best hitters in baseball, with batting averages of .300 to .400, hit safely only three or four times out of every ten times at bat. Time after time they step up to the plate and hit a grounder to an infielder, or fly out to an outfielder, or strike out. They are great batters because their averages are high.

Life often throws tough problems at us. We have to make lightning-fast decisions. Many of us lose interest in the game of life because we fail so often. The great batters will help to give us courage. Although they fail more often than they hit, they always come to bat with the determination to knock the ball over the fence.

If we meet our problems with courage and determination, our averages will break pretty well, too. Remember that great inventors have dozens of failures before they perfect their inventions. Great ball-carriers in football often are stopped for no gain. Great chemists try hundreds of experiments for each important discovery. The great records are made only by those who never stop trying.

warding off the bad results of an evil eye or spirit, and bringing good luck to the person or animal that wore it. It seems that in these islands where the beads were used, if a mere glance from the evil eye of an enemy fell on a person or an animal, it was believed that bad luck, even sometimes to the extent of death, would follow. Hence practically all of the livestock and people wore such strings of beads as mentioned.

It recalls the day when some of us carried buckeyes or a rabbit's foot in our pocket. Or else we hung horseshoes on the barn door, or used a hundred and one other symbols to keep off the evil eye of failure or accident. In baseball, for example, a serious player would never think of stepping on a fielders glove for fear of the bad luck which was bound to follow. A pitcher felt it was a bad omen to strike out the first batter to face him—and so it goes.

Strange and interesting as these superstitions are, I am going to describe a new one which is guaranteed to help every leader and teacher every hour of the day. It will protect health, make you more likeable in all you do, insure greater success in your daily work, and bring you home with a sense of "well done, thou good and faithful servant." Here is a picture of the charm +. I ask you to note that it is not a cross, but a plus sign—the sign that protected the life of Charles Lindbergh on his perilous journey across the sea after he had taken the extra pains to shut himself up in a small sedan and sit at the wheel without rest or sleep for 48 hours, studying the effect upon himself of confinement, vibration and motor lullaby. The same charm that brought popularity and success to Elroy ("Crazy Legs") Hirsch because even when the doctors told him he could never play professional football again because of the loss of muscular coordination due to a head injury, he wouldn't quit.

THE "TOP TEN SAYINGS" OF ALL TIME

1. Do unto others as you would that they should do unto you. (Bible—paraphrase of Matthew and Luke.)

2. Know thyself. (Attributed originally by Plato to Socrates.)

3. Anything that is worth doing at all is worth doing well. (Earl of Chesterfield.)

4. If at first you don't succeed, try, try, again. (William E. Hickson.)

5. The great essentials of happiness are something to do, something to love, and something to hope for. (Unknown.)

6. The only way to have a friend is to be one. (Ralph Waldo Emerson.)

7. As a man thinketh in his heart, so is he. (Bible—Proverbs.)

8. Knowledge is power. (Thomas Hobbes.)

9. Actions speak louder than words. (An ancient proverb, source unknown.)

10. An ounce of prevention is worth a pound of cure. (An old English Proverb.)

—Daniel Starch
"Words to Live By" survey

Scientists have said that the average person uses only about one-tenth of the capacity he brings into mortality. (1 + 1 = 2) ($\frac{1}{10} + \frac{1}{10} = \frac{2}{10}$). But, you'll note, it takes the plus sign to do the trick. As extra hope for those who are discouraged, a little added patience and determination when all seems impossible may turn the advancing army of decay and start the forward march that leads to victory and abounding success.

If there is a leader who is downhearted because of failure to attain his ideals, or a teacher who is just about ready to give up because of continued setbacks and failures, let him remember, as Elbert Hubbard has told us, that the line between failure and success is so fine that often a single effort is all that is needed to bring victory out of apparent defeat.

History tells us that George Washington lost nine battles, but by adding the tenth he won the war and the liberty of our country. Woolworth made a failure of his first three stores, but the plus sign pulled the trick; while Lincoln sustained more defeats than victories, kept adding to his faith and determination until he realized the truly great victory.

And so it is, whatever the battle in which we are engaged—and no doubt all of us have some difficulties to face—better than all the beads and buckeyes or other more modern charms, is the armor on which is painted with our own life's effort, the plus sign, meaning with each crushed hope another hope and stronger faith; with each fall in the road, another trial.

Someone has said: "I am never licked until I give up." And the author of one of our sacred books tells us that to him who overcometh—it doesn't matter where he started in life's race—to him that overcometh shall be given the crown of life. It's the plus sign, the

sign that points always forward and not backward, that recognizes defeat only as an opportunity for further effort in the future—by this sign we lead and conquer!

CHAPTER 10 SELF-TEST

1. During the forthcoming week analyze each of the meetings you attend to see how effective they were in:

   a. starting on time

   b. ending on time

   c. achieving the purpose and

   d. motivating people.

   List what you would do to improve the meetings.

2. What do you consider to be your most positive personal attribute? What personal attribute or characteristic do you feel needs improvement? Jot down your plan of action for the next seven days showing what you intend to do to improve it. (Page 377.)

3. Identify two people whom you know and whom you consider to be very enthusiastic. What is it that makes them act and react the way they do. What can you learn from observing them that will assist you in becoming more enthusiastic? How do you plan to implement their ways? (Page 381.)

INDEX